various types of armour available including the furnishing of harness. At the same time it assessed the land and goods of those able to provide financial support. Apart from this it listed the men available within the guidelines of age and fitness. These are the lists which form the bulk of those mentioned in this Guide and are those which are of prime interest to the genealogist.

The dispute between King and Parliament concerning the command of the Militia led to the establishment of the standing army in the 1660's and the role of the Militia started to change. By now the term Trained Bands began to appear as the men were organised into bands and trained at the expense of the parish. Although some fought well in the initial stages of the Civil War, the next hundred years brought a decline in the efficiency of these Militia units. If the truth be known, the Army *per se* began to attract those most suited to military service and those remaining had neither the inclination nor saw the need to be involved. Similarly there were not enough officers to go round once the regular army had taken first choice. Those remaining had to be drawn from the landed gentry and were of amateur status. This did nothing to enhance its reputation and it often failed to deliver 'when the call came.'

The Duke of Monmouth had no difficulty in dealing with the Militia which first stood in his way after his landing at Lyme Regis in 1685. Although a force of 4,000 was mustered at Axminster ready to oppose him, these amateur soldiers were rendered useless by rumour-induced panic. Indeed half the force is said to have gone over to the enemy. The local aspect of the Militia, however, was highlighted later the same year. Monmouth's advance out of the West Country was thwarted by the presence of the Gloucestershire and Wiltshire Bands blocking his progress by the simple expedient of marching up and down their respective county boundaries.

The first half of the eighteenth century saw the decline and virtual disappearance of the Militia, but the Seven Years' War opened a new chapter in its history. With most of the regular army away on the Continent, civil defence became of prime importance and Parliament endeavoured to reorganise matters. This culminated in an Act of 1757 which established the Militia on an entirely new footing. The progress of events, from 1757 until 1831, and the records they created, are described and listed in the companion Guide, *Militia Lists and Musters, 1757-1876.*

The Militia Ballot was suspended in 1829 (though 1831 lists were prepared). This sounded the death knell of the Militia as it was then formed, but voluntary enlistment continued. From now on, however, it was more closely linked with the regular army but then, of course, the recruit was there because the life appealed to him rather than it being an unavoidable chore. During both of the main conflicts of the second half of the nineteenth century, volunteers from the Militia served alongside the regulars.

The story of the Militia drew to a close just prior to the first World War by its conversion into a Special Reserve – the Territorial Force or Army. As recently as 1942, however, during the Second World War, the Local Defence Volunteers (the L.D.V., later to be called the Home Guard), was introduced on Militia principles and enrolment was imposed on male civilians between the ages of 17 and 62. The long-running and much loved television programme 'Dad's Army' has ensured a knowledge of the type of activity in which the Militia must have engaged throughout its many years of invasion-free existence, of dubious military effect but of undoubted social significance in the lives of our ancestors.

The value of the lists

It must be said from the outset that the value of Muster Rolls and Militia Lists to genealogists is a secondary one compared with the main sources of reference, such as parish registers and wills, but they certainly stand alongside other better known 'tools of the trade'. The earliest can establish in a parish the presence of a named male, within the statutory age scale, many years before the emergence of parish registers. It also establishes the status and standing of the family.

An estimate can also be made of the acreage of the land, where applicable, mentioned in the assessment. The value of freehold land has been estimated in the sixteenth century as 6d. per acre for arable, 1s. for pasture and 1s.6d. for meadow. The extent of the various holdings can be calculated by this rough guide; another little piece in the family history jigsaw.

The later eighteenth and early nineteenth century parish Militia Ballot Lists, described by Sir Mervyn in *Militia Lists and Musters*, provide obvious vital information. If a connection with the Militia itself is established, it is often possible to find references to marriages of Militiamen and the baptism of their children in parishes many miles from home, where their regiments were serving. Inevitably the men met up with and married local girls far away from their home county.

The Public Record Office, Chancery Lane, London

The Muster Rolls and Militia Lists for the British Isles listed in this Guide are to be found throughout the archives of the country, central or local, and to a lesser degree some still are in private muniments. However, for pre-eighteenth century records, the vast majority for England and Wales are in the Public Record Office, Chancery Lane, London; and pre-Union Scottish records are in the Scottish Record Office, Edinburgh. Records at the Public Record Office are to be found in various classes, described below.

The earliest return located is that for 1297, following the Statute of Winchester twelve years earlier. In this ninety Sussex gentlemen were summoned to be in London with horse and armour ready for Military service. The names of the individuals in the armies of Henry V in France, a century or so later, are listed in a modern copy of a contemporary manuscript. But these are not the Muster and Militia lists which are of prime interest to the family historian, for names, without parishes, or at the very least hundreds, are of little interest other than as background information. Undoubtedly the returns of the early to mid sixteenth century are the most useful and, provokingly, the most difficult.

The returns for 1522, when an in-depth valuation of property was made on the pretext of a Muster, survive for several counties, but the years 1539 and 1542 are the most proific. They are detailed at length in the Calendars of the *Letters and Papers of the Reign of Henry VIII* (*L&P*), **14**, Part 1, pp.264-329 and **17**, pp.493-511. Others seem to have been put there for the sake of continuity, for they are undated and classified merely as 'Temp. Henry VIII' (in the reign of Henry VIII).

Unless otherwise stated, the documents are in good condition and the division is by parish within hundred. Any variation to this is noted. Where the documents are calendared in detail, the number of names (shown in round brackets) are as recorded there; others are estimated. Where more than one roll is included under a particular reference the numbers of names are within a range of maximum and minimum.

TUDOR and STUART
MUSTER ROLLS

A Directory of holdings
in the British Isles

Jeremy Gibson and Alan Dell

Federation of Family History Societies

First published by the
Federation of Family History Societies,
c/o The Benson Room, Birmingham and Midland Institute,
Margaret Street, Birmingham B3 3BS, England.

Reprinted with minor amendments, 1991

ISBN 1 872094 01 5

Cover and title page graphics by Linda Haywood.
Cover illustration: Detail from engraving of the London trained bands, 1587, at Sir Philip Sidney's funeral.

Typeset from computer disks prepared by Jeremy Gibson
and printed by Parchment (Oxford) Limited.

> 'John Gilpin was a citizen
> Of credit and renown,
> A train-band captain eke was he,
> Of famous London town.'
>
> *William Cowper.*

ACKNOWLEDGMENTS

Work on compiling this Guide started some years ago, and archivists have as always been generous with time and effort in replying to questionnaires and subsequent enquiries. At the Public Record Office, Chancery Lane, where the bulk of these records are, we have had particular assistance and encouragement, especially from Dr David Crook, whose own knowledge of these records is so great. We hope that this Guide will make their existence better known and increase local acquisition of films as well as transcription and research.

We should like thank too Dr. Ian Beckett, the acknowledged authority on British auxiliary forces; Mr. A.C. Chibnall, editor of the Buckinghamshire Record Society volume of Musters; Sir Mervyn Medlycott, bt., co-author of the companion Guide to *Militia Lists and Musters*; and Mr. T.S. Stoate, whose publications of transcripts of West Country records are an example to the rest; for sharing their knowledge and experience.

With particular areas, we are grateful for help from David Clay and Victor Rosewarne (Derbyshire), Derek Tooke (Norfolk), Jean Cole (Wiltshire), Glyn Parry (N.L.W.) and Sheila and John Rowlands (Wales), and Robin McNee Findlay (Ireland). This reprint incorporates amendments to the Scottish section provided by staff of the Scottish Record Office which, through no fault of theirs, arrived too late for the first printing.

J.S.W.G. and A.D.

PREFACE

As with all Guides in this series, our primary object is to provide precise information on the survival and location of comprehensive or extensive lists of personal names which may be of use in family historical research. Thus administrative records, or lists with severely restricted numbers of names, such as those listing officers only, are omitted. There is no claim to exhaustive or authoritative coverage of the whole field of records engendered by the part-time forces known as the Militia.

The majority of the sixteenth and seventeenth century records, described in this Guide, are in the Public Record Office, Chancery Lane, London. These have been researched by Alan Dell, who has physically examined many hundreds of rolls there. He has also researched the diverse British Library Manuscripts Collection. Some records of these centuries are found in local record offices. Details of these are as provided by archivists, and have rarely been personally examined by us. The origins and types of material are described by Alan Dell. In general these are all *Musters*, rolls or books, though that of 1522 is called a *Military Survey*. They list men either actually called to arms or who would be liable for such a call. Whilst some clearly cover a sizeable proportion of able bodied men, many must list just a tiny number that happen to have been chosen or have enrolled voluntarily. Wherever possible an approximate number of names has been shown in round brackets.

In Scotland there are many pre-Union (1707) *Muster Rolls* amongst individual family collections now in the Scottish Record Office, and other relevant eighteenth century records, particularly around 1745-6. The Militia in Scotland was only re-established in 1797, but from the later eighteenth century and during the Napoleonic wars and thereafter the private collections again include muster rolls and occasionally the census-type records. The listing given is based on a search by myself of the card index catalogue at the Scottish Record Office, but there was no opportunity to examine individual records. In some cases collections may include unidentified lists and, again, further information will be welcomed. It is probable, too, that private Scottish muniments might provide many more lists of interest.

For Ireland there is an important Ulster collection for 1631 in the British Library Manuscripts Collection. A few apparently relevant holdings in Irish repositories are included, based mostly on references in the *Handbook of Irish Genealogy* (Heraldic Artists Ltd., 1973), but have not been personally researched.

Later records of the reconstituted Militia from 1757 on, and various others engendered by the Napoleonic Wars between 1797 and 1815, are described in the companion Guide to *Militia Lists and Musters*.

Jeremy Gibson

INTRODUCTION

Militia, from the Latin 'Miles': a soldier, was the organisation of a local defence force with a semblance of military training.

It originated in this country with the Anglo Saxon Fyrd, a tribal arrangement which demanded military service from every able and free born male. This was expanded by King Alfred who, after the Danes overran the country, sought to prevent a repetition of this tragedy by determining that all males between 15 and 60 should join the general levy or Fyrd and serve for their own Shire.

They were organised locally and were quite temporary in nature, which distinguished them from the professional soldier. When the call came they, or perhaps a proportion of those liable to serve, abandoned their civilian occupations and become soldiers overnight.

This system was augmented by the Statute of Winchester in 1285, which read (Clause 6):

It is likewise commanded that every man have in his house arms for keeping the peace in accordance with the ancient assize; namely that every man between fifteen years and sixty be assessed and sworn to arms according to the amount of his lands and of his chattels; that is to say, for fifteen pounds worth of land, and forty marks worth of chattels, a hauberk, a helmet of iron, a sword, a knife and a horse; for ten pounds worth of land and twenty marks worth of chattels, a haubergeon, a helmet, a sword and a knife; for a hundred shillings worth of land, a doublet, a helmet or iron, a sword and a knife; for forty shillings worth of land and over, up to a hundred shillings worth, a sword, a bow, arrows and a knife; and he that has less than forty shillings worth of land shall be sworn to have scythes, gisarmes, knives and other small weapons. And all other who can do so shall have bows and arrows outside the forests and within them bows and bolts. And that the view of arms be made twice a year. And in each hundred and liberty let two constables be chosen to make the view of arms and the aforesaid constables shall, when the justices assigned to this come to the district, present before them the defaults they have found in arms, in watchkeeping...*etc*.

It continued throughout the Middle Ages alongside the feudal Levy, which was based upon the service of the military fiefs of the King who were summoned, by writ from the Crown, to attend with their retainers.

Sometimes these levies ran alongside each other and local service and overseas wars become intertwined. The seemingly unlawful raising of troops for 'foreign parts' from this Feudal Levy was forbidden by various Acts of Parliament, but the general Levy or Muster, as it had become called, survived. It was also used as a civil force known as the *Posse Comitatus* to quell riots and apprehend wrongdoers.

As time went by the physical attendance at a Muster was discouraged for the authorities were nervous when large numbers of armed men assembled together, for whatever reason. Local routine was also disrupted when men were forced to leave their places of work, particularly at harvest time. Therefore the selection of individuals in any one county was left to the Commissioners of Array who, with the help of county and parish officials, drew up Muster Certificates which listed the

4

The main sources of reference are:

Exchequer. Treasury of Receipt. Miscellaneous Books [E.36].
In addition to their listing in the *Guide to the Public Records*, there is a modern *precis* of the contents, some of which are detailed in *Letters and Papers* (*L&P*) (see above).

Exchequer. Augmentations Office. Miscellaneous Books [E.315].
This covers a return of 1522 of parts of Berkshire, Norfolk and Cornwall.

State Papers Domestic. Henry VIII [SP.1 and SP.2 Case S].
Some of the contents are detailed in *Letters and Papers* (*L&P*) (see above).

All three of these Classes contain former parchment or paper rolls repaired and fixed into leather bound volumes and are generally in good condition and easy to handle. Those in SP.2 Class S are very large and bulky certificates.

Exchequer Accounts. Various [E.101].
These are mostly parchment or paper rolls of varying shapes, sizes and condition. Some are membranes stitched together to form one roll. Others are a series of membranes of differing lengths sewn together at the top. The larger and longer they are, the more difficult they are to handle. Eighty or so are listed by county in *Lists and Indexes* **35**, pp.63-70, but only thirty of these are included in the detailed *Letters and Papers* referred to above. Another 250-odd indenture rolls of Elizabeth's reign are in this class.

State Papers Domestic. Edward VI [SP.10].
A dozen rolls of 1548, some quite small.

State Papers Domestic. Elizabeth [SP.12].
This is a mixed Class. Some, like SP.1, are in volumes. Others are heavy parchment often with seals still attached; some are books of bound papers. Details in the Calendars are vague as to the exact contents, particularly as to whether there are names of men or merely Certificates of Muster.

State Papers Domestic. James I and Charles I [SP.14 and 16].
These are a series of mostly parchment rolls; often just one large sheet with seals attached. Fixed numbers of men (50, 100, 200 and so on) were indented for service for a particular purpose or operation: to serve in Ireland and on the Continent during the Thirty Years War, for example. Indeed there are 70-odd rolls in Class SP.14 listing over nine thousand men to serve in the 1624 expedition of Count Ernst Von Mansfeld, general of the English and French forces for the recovery of the Palatinate. The names represented a small selection of the men of the village, however, whilst the Muster of earlier days listed all the men of the place within the statutory limits. The rolls are well worn and stained but still legible and were probably carried in the field. They are very briefly described in the Calendars.

State Papers Domestic. Supplementry [SP.46/52].
The private papers of John Daniels of Daresbury, detailing his Trained Bands in several hundreds of Cheshire. Late sixteenth century.

Alan Dell

Further Reading

For general background:

Militia Muster Rolls 1522-1640, Public Record Office Information Leaflet **46**, 1986.
Lindsay Boynton, *The Elizabethan Militia 1558-1638*, Routledge and Kegan Paul,
1967; David and Charles, 1971. Very detailed bibliography, extensive footnote
references.
J.R. Western, *The English Militia in the Eighteenth Century: The Story of a Political
Issue, 1660-1802*, Routledge and Kegan Paul, 1965. Extensive footnote
references.
Charles M. Clode, *The Military Forces of the Crown* (2 vols.), 1869, with particular
reference to Statutes governing both the period of this Guide and the subsequent
Militia Lists and Musters.
J.C.K. Cornwall, 'A Tudor Domesday', *Jnl. Soc. Archivists* **3**, 1965.

Dr I.F.W. Beckett has in preparation (for publication by Manchester University
Press, 1990-1) a major study on the British Auxiliary Forces, including the Militia,
Volunteers and Yeomanry for all periods.

Introductions to various record society publications cited under county sections
provide detailed information on their respective sources. In particular the following
are recommended:
A.C. Chibnall, *The Certificate of Muster for Buckinghamshire in 1522*, Bucks.
Record Society **17**, 1973.
J.C.K. Cornwall, *The Military Survey, 1522...for Rutland*, Rutland Record Soceity
1, 1980.
T.R. Stoate, works cited under Cornwall, Devon and Dorset.

BEDFORDSHIRE

Public Record Office, Chancery Lane.

Muster Rolls
1535. Marshead, Flitt, Biggleswade Hds.
(1,500+) [E.101/58/15]. 4m. 5 or 6
columns per page. Closely written, faded
and difficult.
1539. Hds. of **Barford** (174), **Stodden**
(156), **Willey** (246); **Bedford town** (172)
[E.101/59/6]. 4m. See *L&P* **14**, Pt.1,
p.264.
Temp. H.VIII (?1539). Flitt Hd. (300)
[E.36/47].
1597-1600. Eight indenture rolls, by name
and parish (from 16 to 200 per roll)
[E.101/65/13].
1624. Count Mansfeld's expedition. Five
lists: names only (200; 100; 100 (poor);
100; 100) [SP.14/179].
1639. Indenture roll, names only, no
parishes/hds. (80) [SP.16/419].

Bedfordshire Record Office, Bedford.

There is an unpublished TS Guide to *Army
Lists and Muster Rolls at Bedfordshire
County Record Office*, compiled by N.K.
Lutt, 1987 (available for consultation),
which forms the basis (by kind permission)
of the following information.

Muster Lists
c.1685. Entire county (466) [CH.1].
1699. Barford, Stodden and Willey Hds.
(north Beds.). 'Major Harvey's company
mustered at Bedford' (90) [OR.995].

BERKSHIRE

Publications
Muster Certificates: **West Berkshire, 1522**
[P.R.O. E.315/464] in *The Muster*
Certificates for Berkshire, 1522, ed. and
trans. by John Brooks and Nigel Heard.
Oxford Polytechnic, Faculty of Modern
Studies, Occasional Papers **3** (Introduction
and Part 2, 1986), **4** and **5** (Parts 1 and 3,
1987). *Part 1:* **Hds.** of **Shrivenham,
Faringdon** and **Lambourn;** *Part 2:* **Hds.** of
Wantage and **Ganfield;** *Part 3:* **Hds.** of
Faircross, Eagle, Kintbury and **Compton.**
Not indexed.
A separate indexed transcript has been made
by Lis Garnish, copies deposited in the
Berkshire Record Office [T/A 103] and
Oxfordshire Archives, and see 'The Muster
Roll for West Berkshire 1522', by Lis
Garnish, *Oxfordshire Local History*, **2**, 8
(Spring 1988).

Public Record Office, Chancery Lane.

Muster Rolls
1522. West Berkshire [E.315/464]. Book of
131ff. Published.
1569. Hds. and/or **towns** of **Theale** (85),
Reading (215), **Newbury** (120),
Hungerford (10), **Faircross** (150), **Kintbury**
Eagle (50), **Compton** (10), **Wantage** (80),
Shrivenham (100), **Ganfield** (30),
Lambourn (30), **Faringdon** (60), **Homer**
(50), **Ock** (100), **Moreton** (100), **Abingdon**
and **Wallingford** (50), **Cookham** (20), **Bray**
(20), **Ripplesmere** (20), **Sonning** (70),
Charlton (70), **Wargrave** (35), **Beynhurst**
(45) [SP.12/64].
1598. Seven indenture rolls, some by name
and parish, some lists by bands and
commanders (from 35 to 100 per roll)
[E.101/65/14].
1624. Count Mansfeld's expedition. Two
lists, by hd. and parish (200 each)
[SP.14/178].

Berkshire Record Office, Reading.

Trained Bands
1589. Persons liable to serve in **Hurst** and
neighbouring areas [D/EN M49].

BUCKINGHAMSHIRE

Publication

Muster Certificates: **1522, whole county**
(13,000) [Bodleian Library MS Eng Hist
e.187] in *The Certificate of Musters for
Buckinghamshire in 1522*, ed. A.C.
Chibnall, Bucks. Record Society **17** and
R.C.H.Mss. JP **18** (1973). By hd. and
parish. Occupations. Indexed.

Public Record Office, Chancery Lane.

Muster Rolls
1535. Hds. of **Aylesbury** (250/300),
Amersham (350), **Buckingham** (500/600)
[E.101/58/16]. 7m.
1536. Hds. of **Aylesbury** (200), **Ashendon**
(200/250), **Buckingham** (400), **Burnham**
(300), **Cottesloe** (500/550), **Newport**
(700/800) [E/101/59/1]. 28m. Very
unwieldy and highly difficult. Transcript
with Buckinghamshire Archaeological Soc
1548. Aylesbury 3 Hds. (160) [SP.10/3/8].
1587. County, but mostly a summary of
numbers by hd. (600) [SP.12/204]. 8ff.
1590-1601. Twelve indenture rolls by name
and parish (20 to 200 per roll)
[E.101/65/15].
1639. Indenture roll (187 names, only a
proportion of the 200 to be levied; no
place) [SP.16/419].

The British Library Manuscripts Collections.

Muster Rolls
1624-25. Volume headed *Miscell. Bucks.
Musters 1593-1649* [Stowe MSS. 801].
Mostly summaries of numbers by parishes
with hds. but at f.41: copies of indentures
concerning the transport of soldiers
impressed in the county with the lists of
men impressed in **1624** by name and
parish (194); at f.45: list of men indented
in **1625** by name and hd. only (200).
1638, 1660-61. Volume headed *Trained
Bands of co. Bucks. 1660/2* [Stowe MSS.
441]. Starts with a great deal of statistical
information but has:
1638. Cottesloe Hd. and six towns in
Ashendon Hd., provision of horse and foot
soldiers (150) by name and parish
[ff.34-38]; **Newport Hd.:** same (156) plus
substitutes [ff.39-55];
1660. Buckingham Hd. List of provision of
34 horse and 71 foot soldiers by name and
parish and like number of suppliers of same
[ff.26-32];

Buckinghamshire: *British Library* continued

1661. Buckingham. Trained Band of Foot
(90) [f.60].
n.d.. Buckingham 3 Hds. List of Foot levied
as trained bands (100) [ff.95-100].

*Bodleian Library, Dept. of Western
Manuscripts, Oxford.*

Muster Certificates
1522. County (13,000) [MS Eng.hist.e.187;
microfilm at *Bucks. Record Office*].
Published.

Buckinghamshire Record Office, Aylesbury.

Muster Book
1673. Whole county. Arranged by name of
troop or company leader; name and
residence given (300) [L/Md/1/8].

CAMBRIDGESHIRE

Public Record Office, Chancery Lane.

Muster Rolls
1548. Hds. of **Radfield** (50), **Cheveley** (70),
Chilford and **Whittlesford** (60)
[SP.10/3/12]; **Wetherley** (45), **Armingford**
(70), **Stow** (35), **Thriplow** (55)
[SP.10/3/13]; **Staine** (35), **Staploe** (50),
Flendish (20) [SP.10/3/14]; **Isle of Ely** (70)
[SP.10/3/15]. Quite difficult.
1598-1600. Five indenture rolls by name
and parish (from 50 to 100 per roll)
[E.101/65/16]. Very fragile.
1624. Count Mansfeld's expedition (200, by
parish) [SP.14/179].
1626-7. Indenture roll (100, names and
parishes) [SP.16.46].

The British Library Manuscripts Collections.

Muster Rolls
1626-1640. Volume headed *Cambridgeshire
Militia 1626-1640* [Harl. MSS 4014].
Mostly copies of letters and general
instructions from Earl of Suffolk, Lord Lt.,
on behalf of the King to his deputies but at
f.52: Copies of Indenture of 250 soldiers by
parishes in **1639**. Same for 50 soldiers in
1640.

Cambridgeshire Record Office, Cambridge.

Muster Certificates
1597-1601. County [TR.711/1-5,
photocopies of P.R.O. E.101/65/16].

CHESHIRE

Public Record Office, Chancery Lane.

Muster Rolls
1547. Hd. of **Edisbury** (637)
[E.101/549/10]. 18m. Poor. See *L&P* **21**,
Pt. 2, p.205.
1548. Hd. of **Northwich** (400 +)
[SP.10/3/9]. Confusing.
1559. Hds. of **Wirral** (60), **Broxton** (150),
Edisbury (100), **Bucklow** (200),
Macclesfield (200), **Northwich** (200),
Nantwich (200) [SP.12/2]. By hds. only.
Mutilated.
1588, 1596. 'Muster Roll of the Footband of
which John Daniels is the Captain'. **Hds.** of
Bucklow, Macclesfield and **Edisbury** (100
in each) [SP.46/52/138-140].
1588, 1596. 'Muster Roll of the Footband of
which John Daniels is the Captain'. **Hds.** of
Bucklow, Macclesfield and **Edisbury** (100
in each) [SP.46/52/138-140].
1639. Indenture roll by hd. and name (150)
[SP.16/419].
1640. Indenture roll by trained band, hd.
and name (500) [SP.16/462].

Chester City Record Office.

Muster Rolls and Books
*c.*1550-1616. Mayor's Military Papers: men
from Chester and from various English and
Welsh counties. Numbers on rolls mostly in
range 10-60, but some larger, *e.g.* **1602:**
1,500 levied in 20 counties; **1608:** 350
levied in City of London [MMP].

CORNWALL

Publications
Military Survey and Loan: 1522/3, **whole
county** [P.R.O. E.315/77,78] in *Cornwall
Military Survey 1522* ed. T.L. Stoate, 1987.
The survey as such survives for the **Hds.** of
Penwith, Kerrier, Trigg, West and **East.**
Lists of those assessed for the loan, based
on the survey, cover the whole county
except for six parishes in Powder Hd.
(approx. 3,000).
*Muster Roll: c.*1535, **Tinners** [P.R.O.
SP.1/234, E.36/53] in *Cornwall Military
Survey 1522* above. This covers the **Hds.**
or **Stannaries** of **Blakemoor, Foweymoor,
Kerrier, Penwith** and **Tywarnhail** (4,582).

Cornwall: Publications continued

Muster Roll: **1569, whole county** [P.R.O.
SP.12/52] in *Cornwall Muster Roll, 1569,*
ed. H.L. Douch, publ. by T.L. Stoate, 1984.
Comprising **Hds.** of **Lesneth** (963), **Stratton**
(1,033), **Powder** (1,328), **West** (800), **Pyder**
(1,057), **East** (1,622), **Trigg** (1,435), **Kerrier**
(2,210) and **Penwith** (1,947).

Public Record Office, Chancery Lane.

Military Survey and Loan
1522/3. County [E.315/77] (book of 113pp.);
[E.315/78] (book of 65 pages). Published.

Muster Rolls
*c.*1535. Tinners in Stannaries [SP.1/234,
f.255; E.36/53]. Published.
1569. County [SP.12/52] (some lost in Hds.
of Kerrier and Penwith; Hd. of Lesneth very
fragile). Published.
1597-98. Seven indenture rolls, one by
name and parish (from 75 to 100 per roll),
six by names only [E.101/65/18].

Cornwall County Record Office, Truro.

Muster Rolls
1643-44. St. Just in Roseland [DDT.1613].
1671. St. Mawes Castle [DDT.1725].
1715. St. Austell (duplicate muster book)
[DDT.1875]; St. Mellion [DDP.143/1/1];
Gulval [DDML.641].

Devon Record Office, Exeter.

Muster Rolls
1558/9. Hds. of East, West, Powder and
Kirrier [W1258M/E12].

Assessments (for militia?)
n.d. (16th cent.). Hds. of Pydar, Powder,
Trigg, East, West, Stratton, Penwith,
Kerrier [CR.627].

CUMBERLAND

Public Record Office, Chancery Lane.

Muster Rolls
1535. Hds. of **Leath, Eskdale, Allerdale
Above** and **Below, Cumberland**
[E.101/549/13]. One volume of 201 pages,
40 names per page (8,000).
1534. Hds. of **Allerdale Above, Eskdale,
Leath, Allerdale Below** [E.101/61/33]. 42
paper pages of varying length, too difficult
to examine in detail.

Cumberland continued

The British Library Manuscripts Collections.

Muster Roll
1539. 'Names (114) of all the Gentlemen within the Shire of Cumberland and Westmorland, 1539' [Cotton MSS. Calig. B. III, f.192]. See *L&P* 14, Pt. 1, pp.319-20.

Cumbria Record Office, *Carlisle.*

Muster Rolls
n.d. (pre-1623). Horsemen and footmen Nether Crosby, Over Crosby, Brunstock, Walby [D/Lons/L13/6/16.

DERBYSHIRE

Publications
Muster Rolls ('Trained bands'): 1585. Scarsdale and High Peak Hds. (180).
1587. County (400) in *Derbyshire Archaeological Journal*, 17 (1895), pp. 4-25.
1624. Scarsdale Hd. (250, incomplete), in J.P. Yeatman, *Feudal History of Derbyshire*, 2, section 3.
Forthcoming: see *Muster Rolls*, 1638 and 1639, below.

Public Record Office, *Chancery Lane.*

Muster Rolls
1535. Repton and Gresley Hds. (200/250) [E.101/549/1]. 4m..
1536. High Peak Hd. (1,000). Derby w. and town (400/500) [E.101/58/17]. 8m.
1536. Hds. of Appletree (656), Wirksworth (523) [E.101/59/2]. 2m. (parchment sheets 2 ft. x 3 ft.; six columns of names on both sides, very difficult in parts).
1539. Hd. of High Peak (1,124), Derby town (231), Hds. of Scarsdale (1,400), Wirksworth (625), Appletree (532), Morleston and Litchurch (840), Repton and Gresley (300) [E.101/59/7]. 5m. Fading in parts. Difficult to handle due to large size. Detailed at length in *L&P* 14, pt.1, pp.265-7.
1597/1601. Three indenture rolls by names and parish (from 60 to 80 per roll) [E.101.65/19].
1624. Count Mansfeld's expedition. Three lists, by parish and occupation (150; 50; 50) [SP.14/179].

Derbyshire: *P.R.O.: Muster Rolls* continued

1626-7. Indenture roll (50, parish, occupation) [SP.16/46].
1638. Hds. of Scarsdale (4,079), **High Peak** (4,915), **Appletree** (2,080), **Morleston and Litchurch** (2,215), **Wirksworth** (1,910), **Borough of Derby** (657), **Hd. of Repton and Gresley** (1,555) [SP.16/405]. In very good condition, with complete county coverage (17,411 names in all). The 'Trained bands' and those to supply horses were in a separate list which does not survive for this date. Transcribed by V.A. Rosewarne for publication by Derbyshire Record Society, 1991.
1639. Indenture roll by place, name and occupation (200) [SP.16/419]. For publication.
1639. Hds. of Scarsdale (320), **High Peak** (320), **Appletree** (300), **Wirksworth** (230), **Morleston and Litchurch** (230), **Repton and Gresley** (200), **Derby town** (45) [SP.17E/14]. Divided into trained bands, private arms, and those to supply horses (total of 1,645 men and some women). Alphabetical by parish within hds. Only a few men per parish. Complements 1638 muster list. Transcribed and for publication by Derbys. R.S.

The British Library Manuscripts Collections.

1660. 'Letter Book of John Milward, Deputy Lt. of County' [Add.Mss. 34306]. Divided into (a) Trained and (b) Private Soldiers. **Scarsdale** (a: 84; b: 94), **High Peak** (a: 80; b: 79); **Wirksworth** (a: 47; b: 43).

Derbyshire County Record Office, *Matlock.*

Muster Rolls
1573. People able for armour. **Wirksworth** Hd. [D9M Vol.D ff.369-84].
1642-43. Parliamentary Garrison, in Account Book of Nathaniel Halowes [D9M Box 1 f.124]. Large list.
1644. Officers and men [D1232M/0 110].
1645. Lists of soldiers [D1365Z/Z9; D1365Z/Z15- 16].
1647. Horsemen and officers [D1232 M/0 111].
1648. Musters [D1232 M/0 112-13].
1654. Officers and men [D1232 M/0 114].
1659. Commissioned Officers, Officers of horse [D1232 M/0 115-16].

Derbyshire: *C.R.O.: Muster Rolls* continued

1690. Ashbourne Muster. [D258 M/Box 31/10l].
1715. Militia Horsemen (**Wirksworth Hd.**) (140) [D258M Box 30/10ba].

Derbyshire Local Studies Library, Derby.

1621. Hds. of **High Peak, Scarsdale** and **Wirksworth** (part). Trained band and private arms (600) [Kerry vol.19 pp.85-130, transcript of document at Belvoir Castle].

DEVON

Publications
Military Survey: **1522. City of Exeter** (15 parishes) [Devon R.O. E.C.A., Book 156a], in *Tudor Exeter: Tax Assessments 1489-1595*, ed. Margery M. Rowe, Devon & Cornwall Record Society, N.S. **22**, 1977. 1,363 names by parish. Bowmen, Billmen and Not Able. Those with lands within but living without. Aliens.
Muster Rolls: **1569. County** [P.R.O. SP.12/57], as *Devon Muster Rolls for 1569*, ed. A.J. Howard and T.L. Stoate, 1977. By Hd. and parish. 15,000 names, indexed.

Public Record Office, Chancery Lane.

Muster Rolls
1535. City of Exeter (1,000-1,200) [E.101/58/18]. 14m. By parishes. Some difficult. **Hds.** of **Tavistock** (500) [E.101/58/19], 6m.; and **Stanborough** (350-400) [E.101/58/20], 8m.; both difficult, include incapable and impotent men.
1539. Hds. of Roborough (181), **Tavistock** (139), **Lifton** (387) [SP.1/145]. See *L&P* **14**, Pt.1, p.267.
Temp. H.VIII. Hd. of Plympton (only?) (550-600) [E.101/61/34], 5m.
Temp. H.VIII (1539). Hds. of Halberton (150), **Hayridge** (150), **Bampton** (100), **Hemyock** (200), ?**Tiverton** (160) [E.101/61/35]. Difficult.
1569. County (15,000) [SP.12/57]. Published. .
1580. Manor and Town of Bradninch (165) [SP.12/138].
1593-99. Seven indenture rolls, two by name and parish (from 60 to 100 per roll), five by name only [E.101/65/20].

Devon: *P.R.O.: Muster Rolls* continued

1624. Count Mansfeld's expedition. By hd. and parish (100) [SP.14/178]; four lists: by parish and occupation (100); by parish (100; 100; 200) [SP.14/179].
1626-7. Indenture roll (100, parish) [SP.1646].
1638. City of Exeter (4 Quarters of City, Trained Bands) (449); Able men not belonging to same (4 Quarters of City) (919) [SP.16.407].
1640. Five indenture rolls (from 63 to 334 per roll) [SP.16/462].

Devon Record Office, Exeter.

Military Survey
1522. City of Exeter (1,363) [E.C.A., Book 156a]. Published.
1522 also. Parishes of Littleham Landcross, Meeth, Little Torrington, Newton St. Petrock, Beaford, Alwington, Petrockstowe, Shebbear, Buckland Filleigh, Wear Gifford, Merton and Peters Marland [1148 M add/18/5].

Muster Rolls
1569. Hds. of **Hayridge, Tiverton, Bampton, Halberton, Hemyock, Axminster, Colyton, Ottery St. Mary, East Budleigh, Cliston, Wonford, Exminster** and **West Budleigh** [1262M Political 15].
1569. Parish of Broadhempston [63/9, transcript only]. See also published transcript of P.R.O. list.
1691. Parish of Luppitt: foot arms muster [337 B add/MS 24 (641)]; Stowford militia rate [CR.1460].
1697. Parish of Dean Prior: foot soldiers in militia [Z.1/43/6/5]; assessments (horse and foot) for East Allington [Z.143/6/9]; Shobrooke [Z.1/43/8/2]; **West Budleigh Hd.** [Z.1/43/8/1].
1699. Trained soldiers in Sir Francis Drake's Regiment, Devon Militia [Z.1/43/4/1].
n.d. (17th cent.). **East Budleigh Hd.** and others. 'Captain James Huyshes Company' [2530 M/SS/4/1].
1715. Coleridge Hd. [Z.1/43/2/1-9]; **Ermington Hd.** [Z.1/43/3/1-11]; **Lifton Hd.** [Z.1/43/4/2-18]; **Roborough Hd.** [Z.1/43/5/1-12]; **Stanborough Hd.** [Z.1/43/6/1-4, 6-8, 10-22]; **Tavistock** [Z.1/43/7/1-4].

Devon continued

Somerset Record Office, Taunton.

Muster Rolls
Note. The following are all in the Trevelyan
Collection, in files of Lieutenancy Papers for
both Devon and Somerset, all 16th-17th
centuries.
*c.*1620. Coleridge Hd. Trained bands (150)
[DD/WO 56/6].
1633, 1634, 1638, 1639. Hemyock Hd.
(250 each) [DD/WO 53/1, 56/1].
1638. Hemyock Hd. Trained bands (100)
[DD/WO 53/1].
1638-40, *c.*1640. Hemyock Hd. Trained
bands (900 in all) [DD/WO 56/6] (10
documents).
*c.*1640. Hayridge Hd. (100) and
Payhembury parish (60). Trained bands
[DD/WO 56/6].

DORSET

Publication
Muster Rolls: County, 1539 (6,783), 1542
(6,406), 1569 (3,747) [P.R.O. E.36/29,
SP.2/S, E.36/51, E.101/61/36, SP.12/56]
in *Dorset Tudor Muster Rolls 1539, 1542
and 1569,* ed. T.L. Stoate, 1978. Indexed.

Public Record Office, Chancery Lane.

Muster Rolls
1539. County [E.36/29 f.2, f.26; SP.2/S
f.1-43]. Published. See also L&P **14**, Pt. 1,
pp.267-69.
1539 or 1542. County [E.36/17; E.36/29
f.57; E.36/51; E.101/61/36]. Published.
See also *L&P* **17**, pp.493-96.
1569. County [SP.12/56]. Published.
Note. As these rolls are available in an
excellent published edition, no break-down
by hds. and boroughs is included here.
1597-1601. Seven indenture rolls by name
and parish (from 20 to 160 per roll)
[E.101/65/21].
1624. Count Mansfeld's expedition. By hd.
and parish (200) [SP.14/178], bad; by hd.
only (50) [SP.14/179].
1626-7. Indenture rolls (232 by hd.; 94 by
parish) [SP.16/46].

Dorset Record Office, Dorchester.

Muster Rolls
1319. Bridport (176) [B.3/FG.1].
1457. Bridport (202) [B.3/FG.3 and
Ph.694].

Co. DURHAM

Public Record Office, Chancery Lane.

Muster Rolls
1569. Wards of Easington (1,011),
Stockton (953), Chester (1,486),
Darlington (6,477) [SP.12/51].

ESSEX

Public Record Office, Chancery Lane.

Muster Rolls
1536. Uttlesford and Freshwell Hd.
(900-1,000) [E.101/549/8]. 16m.
1539. Barstable Hd. (837) [E.101/59/8],
36pp.; Witham Hd. (a few parishes only)
(37) [SP.1/145, f.9], 2pp. See *L&P* **14**, Pt.
1, p.270.
1592-1601. Fifteen indenture rolls, mostly
by name and parish, one with 300 names
only [E.101/65/22].
1624. Count Mansfeld's expedition. Five
lists, by parish (250; 200; 25 (poor); 200;
100) [SP.14/179].
1626-7. Indenture rolls (60 footmen, part of
72 levied, by parish; 87 by parish)
[SP.16/46].

The British Library Manuscripts Collections.

Muster Rolls
1624-5. Ongar Hd. 'Muster Book of Capt.
Stonner's Band'. June 1624: divided into
types of arms by parish (234 names);
March 1625: the same (135); July 1625
(300). Also includes a list of those who
similarly refuse to find arms; and a list of
20 clergy to find arms [Harl. MSS 7018].
Note. Harl. MSS 6284 appears to be a copy
of part of Harl. MSS 7018.

GLOUCESTERSHIRE and BRISTOL

(for Bristol see also under Somerset)

Publication

Muster Roll: County, 1608 [Glos. R.O.
D.678 Acc. 2798, MF 335] in *Men and
Armour in Gloucestershire*, compiled by
John Smyth or Smith of North Nibley,
pubd. 1902, reprinted by Alan Sutton,
1980. 19,402 names by hd. and parish.
Key to approximate age plus occupation.
1980 edition indexed.

Public Record Office, Chancery Lane.

Muster Rolls

Temp. H.VIII. Tewkesbury Town and Hd.
(300-350) [E.101/61/37]. 7m.

1535. Hds. of St. Briavells (531), Blidesloe
(233), Botloe (469), Westbury (129), and
Duchy of Lancaster (339) [E.101/58/21]
(1542 in ptd. cal.), 28m; Hds. of
Grumbolds Ash (500) and Puckchurch
(71) [E.101/58/24] (1542 in ptd. cal.), 6m.
See *L&P* 17, p.498-9.

1535 also. Slaughter Hd. (300-350)
[E.101/58/22], 7m.; patchy and fading;
Whitstone Hd. (600-700; both able and
unable) [E.101/58/23], 7m.; Kiftsgate Hd.
(250-300) [E.101/58/25], 8m.; Gloucester
Town (350-400), Hds. of Dudstone and
King's Barton (550-600) [E.101/58/26].
8m.

1539. Kiftsgate Hd. (408) [SP.2/S f.45];
Gloucester Town (371), Hds. of Dudstone
and King's Barton (623) [E.101/59/9],
4m.; Hds. of Botloe (381), St. Briavells
(478), Blidesloe (290), Westbury (226)
and Duchy of Lancaster (256)
[E.101/59/10], 11m., fading and patchy;
Hds. of Berkeley (886), Tewkesbury
(337), Tibaldstone (62), Thornbury (369)
[E.101/59/11], 12m., 18 sides, 150-200
per side, crumbling in places. See *L&P* 14,
Pt. 1, p.271-2.

1539 also. Freeholders (3,000 +,
presumably whole county) [E.101/60/2].
18m.

1542. Hds. of Kiftsgate (916), Tibaldstone
(86) [E.36/52 f.1]; Hds. of Whitstone
(923), Bisley (585) [E.36/52 f.22];
Berkeley Hd. (927) [E.101/60/7], 10m.;
Hds. of Cheltenham (200), Deerhurst
(260), ? (120) [E.101/60/8], 9m.; Hds. of
Barton (140), Henbury (262), Thornbury
(324) [E.101/60/9], 11m. See *L&P* 17,
pp.496-8.

P.R.O.: Muster Rolls continued

1547. Hds. of Westbury (114), Botloe
(290), St. Briavells (468), Blidisloe (189)
and Duchy of Lancaster (221)
[E.101/549/11]. 26m. See *L&P* 21, Pt. 2,
pp.205-06.

1591-1602. Twelve indenture rolls, mostly
name and parish (from 40 to 200 per roll).
Two seem much older (lists of hundreds of
men) [E.101/65/23].

1624. Count Mansfeld's expedition. By
occupation (100) or by parish and
occupation (50) [SP.14/178]; by
occupation (100), by names only (40)
[SP.14/179].

1640. Gloucester City (130), indenture roll
[SP.16/462].

Gloucestershire Record Office, Gloucester.
(Daily charge made.)

Muster Rolls

1539. County [D.837: photocopies of
P.R.O. E.101/59/9-11].

1551-2. Military Survey. Hds. of 'Grimbolds
Ash, Tormanton, Lytleton and Acton
Turvyle' [Microfilm MF 1163, 1164 of
Berkeley Castle Muniments: Select Books,
27].

1588, 1595. Gloucester City. Order and
letter book, incl. names of men mustered
(300 in 1588) [GBR H.2/1].

c.1608. Thornbury, Wotton Hd., Berkeley,
Grumbalds Ash. [D.48 Z.6].

1608. County, by Hd. 'Men and Armour in
Gloucestershire, 1608', compiled by John
Smyth of North Nibley [D.678 Acc. 2798
(not available without prior application); MF
335]. Published.

1635. County, in Gloucester City order and
letter book [GBR H.2/2].

HAMPSHIRE

Public Record Office, Chancery Lane.

Muster Rolls

1522. Hds. of Thorngate (180), King's
Somborne (170), City of Winchester
(350), Hds. of Christchurch (430),
Ringwood (100), Fordingbridge (160),
Mansbridge (150), New Forest (120),
Buddlesgate (110), Micheldever (60),
Barton Stacey (60), Holdshot (170),
Pastrow (100), Kingsclere (150), Crondall
(130), Bermondspit (110), Basingstoke
(310), Chuteley (60), Titchfield (includes
Portsmouth, Porchester, Fareham,
Alverstoke and Hamble-le-Rice) (380), L. of
New Alresford (55), Hds. of
Mainsborough (35), Bountisborough (30),
L. of Bishop's Sutton (120), Hds. of
Wherwell (170), Evingar (200), H. and T.
of Andover (360), Hd. of Portsdown and
L. of Finchdean and East Meon (370), Hd.
of Bishop's Waltham (250), Soke of
Winchester (140), Hd. of Odiham (300),
Ls. of Selborne (150), Alton (440), Hds.
of Meonstoke (60), Overton (100),
Fawley (160), Redbridge (80), Town of
Romsey (60) [E.36/19].

1548. Hds. of Portsdown and Bosmere and
T. of Havant (250), Hds. of Titchfield
(75), Fareham (30), Hambledon (30)
[SP.10/3/19].

1569. Winchester City and Liberty of
Stoke (150), Hds. of Andover (160),
Wherwell (80), Thorngate (160), King's
Somborne (180), Barton Stacey (50),
Chuteley (60), Evingar (200), Kingsclere
(140), Overton (130), Pastrow (80),
Basingstoke (150), Crondall (90),
Holdshot (120), Odiham (200),
Micheldever (60), Ls. of Alton (200),
Selborne (80), East Meon (80), Finchdean
(100), Hds. of Bountisborough and
Mainsborough (50), Buddlesgate (150),
Mainsbridge (200); Portsdown (Hd. or
Division?) (400-450); there follow 9 pages
badly mutilated without headings, about
700 men (could be Divisions of New
Forest, East and West) [SP.12/59]. Some
lost on ms. for Alton, Selborne, East Meon,
Finchdean; Mainsbridge and Portsdown
becoming bad.

1593-1601. Five indenture rolls (1 by name,
4 by parish and name, varying from 50 to
100) [E.101/66/10]. Very fragile.

P.R.O.: *Muster Rolls* continued

1624. Count Mansfeld's expedition. Five lists
(names only: 250, 200, 200, 150 and
100) [SP.14/178].

Hampshire Record Office, *Winchester.*

Muster Rolls

Note. Details of particular places not
supplied, as difficult to express succinctly.
Information as provided:

*Years of survival: c.*230 muster rolls, for
1559, 1590-1640 (especially full coverage
for years 1624, 1626, 1628-9, 1631-3,
1637-8).

Area covered: generally hundreds: also
liberties and boroughs, and the city of
Winchester. Returns by hundreds usually
subdivided into tithings or parishes. Each
roll generally includes at least 100 names
[refs. 44M69/G5.XX-XXXV, XLII-XLV;
5M50/1615; Winchester City Archives
(uncatalogued)].

Southampton City Record Office.

Muster Rolls/Books

**1556, 1567, c.1573, 1579, 1583, 1585,
1589.** Southampton [SC.13/2/2-10].

HEREFORDSHIRE

Publication

Militia Assessments: County, 1663 [British Library Harleian 6766 ff.1-188], as 'Herefordshire Militia Assessments, 1663', ed. M.A. Faraday, Royal Historical Society, Camden Fourth Series, 10 (1972), pp.29-185. 7,291 valuations, by hd. and parish.

Public Record Office, Chancery Lane.

Muster Rolls

1539. Hds. of Radlow (600), Grimsworth (514), City of Hereford (346), Hds. of Huntington (314), Stretford (377), Wigmore and Wolphy (918), Webtree (420), Ewias Lacey (214) [E.36/31]. Large bound book. 185pp. (now in E.36 series). See *L&P* 14, Pt. 1, pp.273-75.

1542. Hds. of Stretford (379), Wigmore (320), Grimsworth (264), Huntington (233), Wormelow (417), Radlow (736), Greytree (685), Webtree (289), Ewias Lacey (287), Wolphy (178), Borough of Leominster (273), Hd. of Broxash (595), City of Hereford (236) [E.36/16]. See *L&P* 17, pp.500-03.

temp. H.VIII. Lordship and Borough of Leominster (200-250), Hds. of Broxash(?) (300), Wolphy (100) [E.101/61/38]. 6m. Beginning to crumble.

1597-1601. Five indenture rolls, by name and parish (from 50 to 200 per roll) [E.101/65/24].

1624. Count Mansfeld's expedition. Names only (150) [SP.14/179].

1639. Indenture roll by parish and name (200) [SP.16/419].

1640. Indenture roll by parish and name (150) [SP.16/462].

The British Library Manuscripts Collections.

Men for Irish Service

1598. County (250) [Harl. MSS. 4271, ff.11-13, 17-18, 22].

1599. Similar (50) [f.32].

1600. Similar (75) [ff.39, 45].

Militia Assessments

1663. County (7,291) [Harleian 6766 ff.1-188]. Published.

HERTFORDSHIRE

Public Record Office, Chancery Lane.

Muster Rolls

Temp. H.VIII. Town and Hd. of Hertford (200), Hds. of Braughing (200), ? (200) [E.101/61/39], 3m., muddled; Hds. of Hertford (200-250), Hitchin (200-250), Casio (300), Broadwater (300) [E.101/549/14], paper, 36ss.

1535. Hd. of Edwinstree (300-350) [E.101/58/27]. Paper, 15ss.

1539. Town and Hd. of Hertford (600) [SP.1/145 f.11]. 14m. See *L&P* 14, Pt. 1, p.275.

1573. St. Albans (4 wards) (200) [SP.12/94].

1591-1601. Seven indenture rolls, by name and parish (from 20 to 100 names per roll) [E.101/65/25]. One very fragile, two names only.

1624. Count Mansfeld's expedition. By hd. and parish (200) [SP.14/179].

1626-7. Indenture roll (100 by parish, occupation) [SP.16/46].

1639. Indenture roll, hd., parish and names (110) [SP.16/419].

The British Library Manuscripts Collections.

Muster Roll

1640. 'Muster Book of Co. Hertford 1640': Hds. of Cashio and Dacorum. Four Foot companies of trained soldiers, within companies, then by parish, page index of parishes. Finders of arms, soldier's name and defects (as to arms). Captains Saunders (154), Mayne (149), Sadler (151), Hoo (152) [Harl. MSS. 2285].

Hertfordshire Record Office, Hertford.

Muster Rolls

1583-97. Edwinstree Hd. (arrranged by parishes) (500) [6990].

1602, 1605. Hds. of Edwinstree, Odsey, Braughing and parish of Walkern in Hd. of Broadwater. Arranged by Hd. and parishes within each (*c.*100 in each) [8283, 9531].

1690. Militia mustered at Hertford, under command of Sir John Bucknall (50) [79902].

HUNTINGDONSHIRE

Public Record Office, Chancery Lane.

Muster Rolls
1584. Hds. of **Leightonstone** (300),
Hurstingstone (200), **Toseland** (200),
Norman Cross (200) [SP.12/168].
1585. Soldiers trained by Richard Dyer (163,
by hd. and parish, one or two per parish,
divided into pikemen, archers and qualifiers
(?), **Hds.** of **Leightonstone** (22, 27, 42)
and **Norman Cross** (19, 18, 35)
[SP.12/182].
1595, 1601. Six indenture rolls, 2 by hd.,
parish and name, 4 by parish and name
(from 25 to 100 per roll) [E.101/65/26].
Some fragile.

Huntingdon Branch, Cambridgeshire
County Record Office.

Muster Rolls
1595, 1601. Photocopies of P.R.O.
E.101/65/26 [2474/1-6].
1715/6. Militia of Horse [M.80/9].
1716. Providers of horses, by hd.
[M.80/12-13, 19-20].

KENT

Public Record Office, Chancery Lane.

Muster Rolls
Temp. H.VIII. Hd. of **Wilmington, Town of**
Dartford (100), **Hds.** of **Sutton** (200),
Lessness (120), **Blackheath** (240), **Bexley**
(250), **Bromley and Beckenham** (80)
[E.101/61/40].
1598. Four indenture rolls by names and
parish (from 50 to 100 names per roll, but
some only 1 or 2 names per parish)
[E.101/65/27].
1624. Count Mansfeld's expedition. Probably
Kent. By parish and occupation (100)
[SP.14/178], poor; by names only (250)
[SP.14/179].
1639. Indenture roll, hds. and names
(1,000) [SP.16/419].

The British Library Manuscripts Collections.

Muster Rolls
1548-49. Lathe of Scray (part): Milton
(250-300; 100) Teynham (75; 25),
Faversham (200; 90), Boughton under
Blean (50; 50) [Add. MSS. 37668, ff.3-10,
31-33].

Kent: *British Library: Muster Rolls* contd.

1638. Lathe of St. Augustine, City of
Canterbury. Light Horse under command
of Sir Thomas Palmer (80 gentlemen within
hds. only) [Harl. MSS. 2192, f.35].
1643. Hds. of **Downhamford** (88) and
Kingshamford (66). Parish and name
and/or substitute [Harl. MSS. 2192, f.76].

Kent Archives Office, Maidstone.

Muster Rolls
*c.*1415. Calehill Hd. [0386 03/1].
1569-1759. New and Old Romney borough.
50 rolls (*c.*5,300 names in all) [NR/CPM
1/1-50].
1574. Queenborough (26 names, transcript
in catalogue) [Qb/ZB.6].
1570-95. Faversham. Thirteen rolls (5,850
names) [Fa/CPm 1-22].
1581. Lathe of Aylesford. Assessment for
Light Horse (51) [U.48 04/1].
1590. Those to provide Light Horse for Mr.
Twisden's band [U.48 04/3].
1615. Tenterden [Te/ZB/1-6].
*c.*1630. Borough of Sandpet in Charing
(men warned to appear) [U.1107 07/2].
1663, 1667. Tenterden [Te/ZB.3/1].
1681, 1683. Sandwich. Arranged by wards
[Sa/ALI/1].
*c.*1690. Ickham, Littlebourne, Stodmarsh
and Wickhambreaux [U.22 01].
1712, 1715, 1718, 1722, 1759.
Sandwich. Arranged by wards [Sa/ALI/2].

Kent Archives Office, Sevenoaks.

Muster Rolls
1700. Lathe of Aylesford. List of troops of
horse [U.1007 017].
1705. Riverhead, Shoreham, Chevening,
Sundridge, Otford, Sevenoaks, Kemsing,
Leigh, Speldhurst, Halstead, Seal [U.1007
018/2-4].

Canterbury Cathedral, City and Diocesan
Record Office.

Muster Rolls
*c.*1580-1618. Canterbury. Trained band
and City watch (*c.*200 each, some listed by
wards), 41 documents.
*c.*1700. Men distributed among inns in
Canterbury.

LANCASHIRE

Publications

The Lancashire Lieutenancy under the Tudors... Pt. 1 (1553-1594)...and Stuarts Pt. 2 (1603-1642), ed. John Harland, Chetham Soc. O.S. **49, 50** (1859). **Hds. of Leyland, Derby, Salford, Blackburn.** Numerous musters, only a few names in each case.

'The Lancashire Militia, 1660-1688', D.P. Carter, in Transactions of the Historic Society of Lancashire and Cheshire (1982).

Public Record Office, Chancery Lane.

Muster Rolls

1569. Hds. of West Derby (1,200-1,300), **Leyland** (400-450), **Blackburn** (700-750), **Amounderness** (750-800), **Lonsdale** (950-1,000), **Salford** (700-750, names within hd. only) [SP.12/58].

Note. The 1569 rolls are being transcribed by Douglas Browning (PO Box 1007, Ringwood, Vic. 3134, Australia), hopefully for eventual publication.

1597-1601. Six indenture rolls, 3 by hd., parish and name, 2 by parish and name, 1 by names only (from 30 to 120 per roll) [E.101/65/28].

1626-7. Indenture roll (200, names only) [SP.16/46].

1639. Indenture roll by hd. and name (250) [SP.16/419].

The British Library Manuscripts Collections.

Muster Rolls

1619-26. West Derby Hd. Muster roll of arms by name and parish [Add. MSS. 36924]. **1619** (150) [ff.6-8]; **1620** (150-200) [ff.10-12]; **1624** (200) [ff.14-15]; **1625** (200) [ff.18-20]; **1626** (200) [ff.24-25].

LEICESTERSHIRE

Public Record Office, Chancery Lane.

Muster Rolls

Temp. H.VIII. Hds. of Gartree (500-50), **Goscott West** (400-50), **Goscott East** (200) [E.101/549/15]. Paper, 38ss.

1539. Hd. of Framland (400+) [SP.1/145 f.20], much mutilated; **Hd. of Goscott** (540) [SP.2/S], 3m. See L&P **14**, Pt. 1, p.275-6.

1569. Hds. of Gartree (150), **East Goscote** (115), **Framland** (120), **West Goscote** (100), **Guthlaxton** (120), **Sparkenhoe** (150), **Town of Leicester** (40) (hd. and names only) [SP.12/65].

1595-98. Four indenture rolls (from 30 to 100 per roll), 2 by parish and name, 2 by names only [E.101/60/29].

1624. Count Mansfeld's expedition. Two lists, by hd. and parish (200 in each) [SP.14/178].

1626-7. Indenture rolls (150, residence and calling; 120, parish and occupation) [SP.16/46].

1640. Indenture roll (400), parish, name, occupation [SP.16/462].

Leicestershire Record Office, Leicester.

Muster Rolls

1579, 1580, 1588, 1608. Borough of Leicester [BR/II/12/5, 7, 9, 14a].

1638. Gartree Hd. 'Men pressed', names, occupations, parishes [DG.5/896]; trained soldiers under Capt. John Roos [DG.5/899, 901].

c.1640. Hds. of East Goscote, Sparkenhoe, Goodlaxton, West Goscote, Gartree; 'The Clergies List under Col. Brookes'; 'Sir Thos. Hartop, Lt. Col.' [DG.5/900, 902-8, 911].

Militia Muster Rolls

1715. County, by hd. and parish (several hundred names) [LM/2/4].

LINCOLNSHIRE

Public Record Office, Chancery Lane.

Muster Rolls

1539. Wapentakes of Hill (200),
Candleshoe (480), **Soke of Bolingbroke**
(400), **Calceworth W.** (445) [E.36/21], a
difficult hand; **Yarborough W.** (330)
[SP.1/145 f.34]; **Haverstoe W.** (200)
[SP.1/145 f.43]; **Soke of Horncastle**
(256), **Gartree W.** (480) [SP.1/145 f.47];
Wraggoe W.(300) [SP.1/145 f.61], some
mutilated; **Aslacoe W.** (100) [SP.1/145
f.68], pretty useless; **Lawress W.** (360)
[E.101/59/12], 2m; **Well W.** (190)
[E.101/59/13], paper, 4pp; **Walshcroft W.**
(550) [E.101/59/14], 3m. See *L&P* **14**, Pt.
1, pp.276-9.

1542. Ws. of Louth Eske (544),
Ludborough (92) [SP.1/173 f.84]. See *L&P*
17, p.503.

1569. Ws. of Louth Eske (550),
Calceworth (450), **Hill** (70) [SP.12/51];
Ws. of Skirbeck (220), **Elloe** (300), **Kirton**
(350-400), **Borough of Boston** (150),
Holland(?) (250) [SP.12/64], double sided
parchment, too difficult to count in detail.

1585. Town of Stamford with **St. Martin's**
(235, usual categories plus farriers,
sharpshooters, masons and smiths), **Ws.** of
Yarborough (300-350), **Bradley** (200),
Lovedon (600, incl. 'pioners'), **Boothby**
Graffoe (470), **Aveland** (300-50, fading,
some lost), **Louth** (300, not by parish but
this given against name), **Ness** (380-400),
Soke of Grantham (450) [SP.12/181]; **W.**
of Winnibriggs and Threo (370, some
lost), freeholders of same (80, bad gaps)
[SP.12/182].

1586. Holland: Ws. of Elloe (500, some
occupations), **Skirbeck** (700), **Skirton**
(330) [SP.12/193.

1624. Count Mansfeld's expedition. By
wapentake, parish and occupation (250)
[SP.14/178].

LONDON and MIDDLESEX

Publications

Muster Rolls: **1611-82.** *The 'Vellum Book'*
of the Honourable Artillery Company, ed.
G.A. Raikes, 1888.

1622-1806. 'Huguenots in Trained Bands of
London and the Honourable Artillery
Company' [from Hon. Artillery Co. MSS.],
in *Proceedings of the Huguenot Society of*
London, **15** (1955), pp.300-16. Lists men
alphabetically with brief biography.

Public Record Office, Chancery Lane.

Muster Rolls

1539. City of London. List of men only
(300+, bowmen and pikemen) [SP.1/242
f.236]; fragment of muster book, names of
bowmen and pikemen listed under trades
(254) [SP.1/242, f.242]. See *L&P*
Addenda 1509-47, Pt. II, p.481.

1542. Middlesex: Hds. of **Isleworth** and
Gore. Names of householders and servants
able to serve the King in several parishes
(250-300) [E.101/61/17]. Paper, 10pp.
Much struck out.

1569. Middlesex: Hds. of Ossulton
(6,000+, incl. St. Margaret's Westminster,
St. Martin in the Fields, St. Giles in the
Fields Marylebone, Hackney, *etc.*), **Elthorne**
(700-750), **Spelthorne** (600-50), **Isleworth**
(200-50), **Gore** (400-500), **Edmonton**
(600-50) [SP.12/64]. Fading badly.
Transcript in progress by V.A. Rosewarne
(15 Ryecroft Avenue, Whitton,
Twickenham TW2 6HH) for eventual
publication.

1590-1601. Middlesex. Six indenture rolls,
1 unreadable, 4 by name, 1 by name and
parish (incl. birthplace and imprest for 50
men) (from 50 to 100 per roll)
[E.101/66/1]; **City of London,** by wards
(30 paper ss., from 130 to 400 names per
sheet) [E.101/66/2], some very fragile.

1624. London. Count Mansfeld's expedition.
Four lists, names only (250; 200; 200;
2000 [SP.14/179].

Greater London Record Office, 40
Northampton Road, EC1R 0HB.

Muster Rolls

*c.***1338. Middlesex.** 'Footmen, being the
return to a Commission of Array', covering
Hds. of Elthorne, Spelthorne, Isleworth,
Gore, Edmonton, Ossulstone, arranged by
parishes (1,000 names, 800 of them for
Spelthorne) [Acc. 1085/FP9].

London and Middlesex continued

Guildhall Library, Dept.of Manuscripts.

Muster Rolls
London: St. Ann Blackfriars (ward of
Farringdon within). **1682, 1685, 1696,
1701, 1724.** Trained bands *etc.*
[Ms. 2096-99].
1683-4. London: St. Bride Fleet Street.
Trained bands [Ms. 6608].

Honourable Artillery Company Archives,
*Armoury House, City Road, London EC1Y
2BQ.*

The Honourable Artillery Company was
embodied in 1537, as the Guild or
Fraternity of St. George, by Letters Patent.
Sadly the early Muster Rolls were lost
during the Civil War. The Artillery Company
was reorganised from 1608 and its Muster
Roll (known as the 'Vellum Book') starts in
1611 and continues to 1682 (published).
From 1682 to date the Muster Rolls are
complete. The list of Members was printed
from the late 18th century on, but until
1862 only the officers were listed. As usally
both work and home address was given,
these can be a valuable source. They are
available in the Guildhall Library to 1945.
The original musters are being indexed with
the aim of producing a single consolidated
index, 1537-1907, but will not be
completed for many years. A total of about
30,000 names are covered by these
sources.
For a small fee and s.a.e. information can be
supplied about Members, to those tracing
ancestors who served in the Company. No
detailed research can be done as the
Archivist is part-time and heavily
committed. No personal research may be
undertaken.
Being a volunteer regiment, few personal
details are available apart from height and
age, birth dates are rarely known and age
has to be taken on trust.

See also under Cheshire: Chester City Record
Office.

Monmouthshire – *see with* **Wales.**

NORFOLK

Publications
Muster Rolls: **1355. City of Norwich Militia,
Arms and Array** [City Archives] in Norfolk
and Norwich Archaeological Society **14**
(1901), pp.263-320. Leets of Conesford,
Mancroft, Wymer and Over the Water. Incl.
long preamble 'Norwich Militia in the 14th
century'.
*c.*1523. **Hd. of North Greenloe** [P.R.O.
E.315/466, bound with Holt], in Norfolk
Record Society **1** (1931), pp.41-68. 141
men plus valuation.
*c.*1523. **Hd. of Holt** [P.R.O. E.315/466,
bound with North Greenloe] in N. & N.A.S.
22 (1926), pp.45-58. 183 able men
(extracts only, but lists clergy).
1569-77 [N.R.O. Bradfer Lawrence IIe], *The
Musters Returns for divers hundreds...*,
transcribed by Miss M.A. Farrow, Pt. 1, ed.
H.L. Bradfer-Lawrence; Pt. 2, ed. Percy
Millican; N.R.S. **6, 7** (1935, 1936). Covers
**Clackrose, 1569; Kings Lynn and
Clackrose, 1572; Town of Thetford, Hds.
of Giltcross and Shropham, 1574; Kings
Lynn and 15 hds., 1577** (5,000 +
names).
1621. Walloon Militia List, in *The Walloons
and their church at* **Norwich**, ed. W.J.C.
Moens, Huguenot Soc. **1** (1887-8),
pp.225-6 [original then in possession of
editor]. 90 names.
1627. State papers relating to Musters, from
*Original Papers of the Norfolk and Norwich
Archaeological Society* (1907), pp. 65-68,
92-96. By hd., but only a few each (386
names) [original MSS then in library of W.
Rye].
1683/4. 'Muster Roll – **East and West
Flegg'** [N.R.O. MS Ref. Petre 1100/1 506
X 9], transcribed by Derek Tooke, in *The
Norfolk Ancestor* **3**, Pt. 9 (June 1985),
pp.124-26.

Public Record Office, *Chancery Lane.*

Muster Rolls
1522. Hds. of North Greenloe (141), **Holt**
(183) [E.315/466]. Also long valuation.
Published.
1524? South Erpingham Hd. (500-700)
[E.101/61/16]. Book of 98 pages, 'Names
of persons for the War', incl. long
valuation.
1536. City of Norwich (500-600)
[E.101/59/3]. 3m.

Norfolk: *P.R.O.: Muster Rolls* continued

Temp. H.VIII. Hds. of South Walsham and Gallow (100), **Brothercross** (230), **City of Norwich** (cal. as **1539**; 720) [E.36/22]. Difficult. A great deal is valuation numbers. Able only. See *L&P* **14**, Pt. 1, p.280.

Temp. H.VIII. Town of Yarmouth (650), **Hds. of West Flegg** (400), **East Flegg** (300), **Tunstead** (800), **Happing** (700) [E.36/25].

1598-1601. Seven indenture rolls, by parish and name (from 50 to 200 per roll) [E.101/66/4].

1627. Indenture roll (250, by parish, some marked 'out of ye gaole') delivered to Peter Murford, Conductor [SP.16/72]. Purpose obscure.

The British Library Manuscripts Collections.

Certificate of Muster
1539. Eynesford Hd., by parish (900-1,000) [Add.Mss. 36936]. 9ff.

Norfolk Record Office, Norwich.

Muster Rolls
*c.*1452. **Norwich City,** by ward (500) [Old Free Book f.20d. Norwich City Records, case 17(c)1].

temp. H.VIII – *c.*1630. **Norwich City,** by ward and parish (*c.*50,000) [Norwich City Records, case 13(a)2].

1569-77. Various hundreds, Kings Lynn, Thetford [Bradfer Lawrence IIe]. Published.

1599. Various hundreds (300; by hd.) [MS 2644, 3 A 2].

1599-1602. Various hds. (1,000; most by hd., some by parish within hd. [WLS XVII/1. 410 x 5].

17th cent. South Rainham parish (10) [MS 1510, 1 D 2].

1601. Holt Hd. (200; by parish) [MS 2649, 3 A 2].

1627. County (150; by hd. and parish within each hd.) [WLS XVII/2, 410 x 5]. Unfit for production

1662. County (1,500; by hd. and parish within each hd.) [Bradfer Lawrence V (X19 and X27)].

1679. Tunstead Hd. (300; by parish) [MS 10275, 35 B 1]. Not fit for production.

Muster Rolls continued

1683/4, 1690, 1700 and three undated. **East and West Flegg** (500) [Pet 1100/1-3, 5, 6, 8, 506 x 9]. 1683/4 published. One other (undated) [1100/5] transcribed and indexed; available in Norwich Local Studies Library and Society of Genealogists. Transcripts of others in progress, by Derek Tooke, Mount Vale, 1 Woodside Close, Caterham, Surrey CR3 6AU.

1691-97. Earsham Half Hd. (200; by parish) [MS 2665, 3 A 3].

1716. South Erpingham Hd. (50; by parish) [MS18134, 77 x 6].

NORTHAMPTONSHIRE

Publications
Muster Rolls: **1540/1.** 'Book of Musters', from MS. in possession of Joseph Mayer (100), in *Northamptonshire Antiquarian Memoranda* **4** (*Northampton Mercury* 6 March 1876).

1588. Eastern Division, incl. Soke of Peterborough. Soldiers under Captains Brown and Niccolles (302), in *Northamptonshire Lieutenancy Papers...1580-1614,* ed. Jeremy Goring and Joan Wake, Northamptonshire Record Society **27** (1975), pp.64-65. Index. This book supplements N.R.S. **3** and **7,** below, and has much of relevance to the Militia, though other lists of names are confined to landowners and borough representatives.
'The Army of Queen Elizabeth, 1588', from collection of State Papers 1571-96, transcribed by William Murdin, *Northamptonshire Antiquarian Memoranda,* **2** (offprint based on article in *Northampton Mercury*).

1591 for **Northampton town,** ten southern hds. of **Spelhoe, Nobottle Grove, Wymersley, Kings Sutton, Cleyley, Greens Norton, Towcester, Guilsborough, Fawsley, Chipping Warden** (1,548 names); and **1612:** Trained Bands, by parish within hd. (Muster Book of Sir Richard Knightley of Fawsley; 1,548 names), in *...Musters, Beacons, Subsidies etc. in the county of Northampton, 1586-1623,* ed. Joan Wake, N.R.S. **3** (1926). Introduction by Dr J.E. Morris traces the development of the militia from the Middle Ages and describes local action taken during the Armada crisis.

Northamptonshire: *Publications* continued

1605, 1613-19. Five of the ten eastern hds.; **1617** for all ten hds. (supplementing the above) [MSS at Boughton House], in *The Montagu Musters Book*, ed. Joan Wake, N.R.S. **7** (1935).

1662. The Northamptonshire Volunteers under the command of the Earl of Westmorland, in *State Papers Domestic Charles II*, **26**, 74 and 75.

Public Record Office, *Chancery Lane*.

Muster Rolls

1539. Hds. of **Guilsborough** (263) [E.101/59/15], 5m.; **Rothwell** (121) [/16], 5m.; **Higham Ferrers** (85) [/17], 2m.; **Hamfordshoe** (28) [/18], 2m.; **Huxloe** (165) [/19], 2m.; **Orlingbury** (68), **Peterborough Liberty** (245), **Polebrook and Navisford** (148) [/20], 5m.; Hds. of **Fawsley** (315), **Nobottle Grove** (170), **Corby** (652), **Willybrook** (254) [E.36/47 f.5,8]; Hds. of **Greens Norton** (180), **Chipping Warden** (115), **Kings Sutton** (309) [E.36/55A f.1]; Hds. of **Spelhoe** (81), **Wymersley** (137) [E.36/55A f.16]. See *L&P* **14**, Pt. 1, pp.280-83.

1542. Hd. of **Guilsborough** (362) [E.36/55A, f.12]; Hds. of **Kings Sutton** (300; mostly good, some lost), **Chipping Warden** (200), **Greens Norton** (100; one third lost), **Towcester** (70; mostly lost) [SP.1/173 ff.94-119]. See *L&P* **17**, pp. 503-05.

Temp. H.VIII. Hd. of (probably) **Towcester** (20 parishes; 250-300) [E.101/549/16]. Paper, 10pp.

1590-1601. Fifteen indenture rolls (by name and parish) [E.101/66/5]. Too fragile to examine in detail.

1624. Count Mansfeld's expedition. Two lists, by parish (100 each) [SP.14/178]; four lists, by parish (50; 25; 25, with occupations; 250 [SP.14/179].

1639. Hds. of **Navisford** (177), **Corby** (200), **Polebrook** (80), **Willybrook** (100), **Navisford** (50), **Higham Ferrers** (50), **Huxloe** (220), **Orlingbury** (20), **Hamfordshoe** (50), **Rothwell** (150) [SP.17/E]. Names only, but parish given against them.

1640. Indenture roll, **Northampton East** (parish and name; 248) [SP.16/462].

The British Library Manuscripts Collections.

Muster Roll

1625. Names of a levy of 100 men to Plymouth [Add.Mss. 34217 f.15]. By name, parish and occupation.

Northamptonshire Record Office, *Northampton*.

Militia Muster Rolls

*c.***1590.** Centre and north of county (excl. Soke of Peterborough) (2,500) [Montagu of Boughton papers]. Undated list; indexed.

1664, 1667, 1678. Musters (50+ each) [Samwell (Upton) Collection S.6, 8, 7].

1679. Brackley, Wellingborough; also General Muster, **1681** (50+) [Samwell (Upton) Collection S.2].

1683. Musters book (part) (50+) [S.11].

1686. Musters (900) [S.13].

1690. Militia Foot at Northampton; Brackley, Oundle, Towcester (50+) [S.4].

NORTHUMBERLAND

Publications

Muster Rolls: **1539.** 'Fencible Inhabitants of **Newcastle upon Tyne**' (874) [P.R.O. SP.1/145], in *Archaeologia Aeliana*, 1st series, **4**, Pt. 2 (1852), pp.119-40. 'Muster for Ward of **Coquetdale and Bambrough** (part) (Alnwick)' (1,530) [P.R.O. E.36/40], in *A.A.*, 1st series, **4**, Pt. 3 (1854), pp.157-201.

Public Record Office, *Chancery Lane*.

Muster Rolls

1539. Town of Newcastle-upon-Tyne (874, but numbers seem at variance with Calendar; by wards; incl. mariners and poor men unable to buy harness) [SP.1/145], published; **Coquetdale and Bambrough Ward** (part) (Alnwick) (1,530) [E.36/40 f.1], published; **Bambrough Ward** (part, incl. Berwick and Bambrough) (440) [E.36/40 f.21]; **Tindale Ward** (Hexham) (3,000+) [E.36/40 f.30]; **Glendale Ward** (Wooler and Eglingham) (1,528; incl. 231 Scotsmen) [E.36/40 f.66]. See *L&P* **14**, Pt. 1, pp.283-86.

1596. Light horse men (allowed and disallowed) (300) [SP.12/256].

Northumberland continued

Northumberland County Record Office, *North Gosforth.*

Muster Rolls
1538/9. Coquetdale and Tynedale Wards,
arranged by parish within each ward.
Transcript of P.R.O. E.36/40 f.1 [ZAN.
M.13/D.15].
1745. Hexham militia rolls for the North
Tyne, South Tyne and Hexharn companies
(200 names, by company) [ZAL. 98/5].

NOTTINGHAMSHIRE

Note. The terms 'Hundred' and 'Wapentake'
appear to be used interchangeably in this
county. For convenience, we have
standardised on 'Hd.'

Publication
Muster Roll: **1595. Newark Hd.** (150
names) [Newark Corporation Minute Book
1] in *Transactions of the Thoroton Society*
10 (1906-7) pp.77-82.

Public Record Office, Chancery Lane.

Muster Rolls
**Temp. H.VIII. Liberty of Southwell and
Scroody.** (600-700) [E.101/62/1], 7m.;
Bassetlaw Hd.(?) (300) [E.101/549/17],
4m; **Broxtow Hd.**(600-700)
[E.101/549/18], 12 paper ss.
1535. Unknown area. [E.101/549/2]. 13m.
1539. Rushcliff Hd. (332) [SP.2/S]; **Hds.** of
Bassetlaw (870), **Broxtow** (650) [E.36/47
f.17]; **Nottingham town** (284) [E.36/47
f.47]. See *L&P* **14**, Pt. 1, pp.286-7.
1542. Bassetlaw Hd. (785) [E.101/62/2],
9m.; **Bingham Hd.** (522) [SP.1/173
ff.122-32]; **Thurgarton Hd.** (864)
[ff.134-46]; **Newark town** (288)
[ff.147-58]. See *L&P* **17** pp.505-6.
1569. Hds. of **Broxstow, Bingham** and
Rushcliff (90-100) [SP.12/54], some
fading; **Hds.** of **Bassetlaw** (550-600),
Newark and Thurgarton (200) [SP.12/62];
Town of Nottingham (105) [SP.12/65].
1590-1601. Nine indenture rolls (7 by hd.,
name and parish, 1 by name, 1
unreadable; from 60 to 100 per roll)
[E.101/66/6].
1626-7. Indenture roll (100, by parish)
[SP.16/72].
1640. Indenture roll (300, parish)
[SP.16/462].

Nottinghamshire Archives Office, *Nottingham.*

Muster Rolls
1605-38. Lists of men [CA.7487-93].
1695. List of garrison at Portland Castle
[DD.4P 66/10].

OXFORDSHIRE

Forthcoming publication
Muster Rolls: **1538, 1542. Hds.** of
Bampton, Bullingdon, Chadlington and
Wootton [P.R.O. E.36/28, E.101/60/11,
SP.1/173] (1,448), transcribed by Peter
Beauchamp for publication by Oxfordshire
Record Society.

Public Record Office, Chancery Lane.

Muster Rolls
1538. Bullingdon Hd. (614) [E.36/28]. For
publication.
1542. Wootton Hd. (249) [SP.1/173
ff.159-62]; **Hds.** of **Chadlington** (294),
Bampton (291) [E.101/60/11]. See *L&P*
17, pp.506-7. For publication.
1569. County (except City of Oxford),
comprising Hds. of Banbury (100),
Bloxham (70), Chadlington (220), Bampton
(140), Wootton (300), Ploughley (220),
Bullingdon (200), Dorchester (125), Thame
(130), Lewknor (120), Ewelme (110),
Langtree (50), Binfield (80), Pirton (50),
Town of Henley (170) [SP.12/65 ff.39-54].
Names by hd. only. Fading in parts. Partial
transcription by and in possession of
J.S.W. Gibson.
1590-1601. Five indenture rolls (4 by hd.,
parish and names; 1 by name; from 25 to
100 per roll) [E.101/66/7].
1624. Count Mansfeld's expedition. By hd.,
parish and occupation (100); by occupation
only (50) [SP.14/178].

RUTLAND

Publication
Military Survey: **1522. County** [P.R.O.
E.36/54 (part only) and E.36/55], in *The
Military Survey of 1522 and the County
Community under King Henry VIII*, ed.
J.C.K. Cornwall, Rutland Record Society **1**
(1980).

Public Record Office, Chancery Lane.

Muster Rolls or Military Survey
1522. Hds. of **Martinsley** (400), **Oakham
Soke** (600), **Alstoe** (300), **Wrandike**
(500), **East** (300) [E.36/55]. Mutilated,
very difficult [also E.36/54, a partial
incomplete copy of E.36/55 of a later date,
*c.*1700]. Published.
1624. Count Mansfeld's expedition. By
parish and occupation (50) [SP.14/178].
1640. County. Indenture roll (60, by parish
and occupation) [SP.16/462].

SHROPSHIRE

Publications
Muster Rolls: **1539. South and North
Bradford Hds.** [P.R.O. E.36/48 f.1 (part
only); SP.2/S f.67 *et seq.* (part only)] in
*Transactions of Shropshire Archaeological
and Natural History Soc.* **8** (3rd Series)
(1908), pp.248-51, 255-75.
1542. Munslow Hd. (incorrectly dated
1532), **Ludlow Borough, Purslow Hd.**
[P.R.O. E.36/48] in *Trans. S.A. & N.H.
Soc.* **8**, pp.251-55.
1579. Town of Shrewsbury (1,195) and
Liberties (573) [Shropshire R.O.
3365/2545] in *Trans. S.A. & N.H. Soc.* **2**
(2nd Series) (1890), p.257. Lists by wards,
occupations with servants thereof. Also
those 'Free of noe occupation.'

Shropshire continued

Public Record Office, Chancery Lane.

Muster Rolls
1539. Bradford South Hd. (734) [E.36/48
f.1]; **Bradford North Hd.** (1,012) [SP.2/S
f.67.]. Published. See also *L&P* **14**, Pt. 1,
pp.287-8.
1542. Bradford Hd. (1,350) [SP.1/173
ff.165-86]; **Munslow Hd.** (1,276) [E.36/48
f.33]; **Ludlow Town** (230; occupations),
Purslow Hd. (355), also Bishop's Lands(?)
(in Purslow; probably Bishop's Castle)
(147; difficult); **Overs Hd.** (147) [E.36/48].
See *L&P* **17**, pp.507-9. Part published.
Temp. H.VIII. Probably **Wenlock Hd.** only
(1,000) [E.101/62/3]. 5m. Fading and
difficult.
Temp. H.VIII. Bradford South Hd. (?;
location doubtful) [E.101/549/19]. 39
loose paper ss., some only scraps.
1597. Indenture roll, by hd. and name (100)
[E.101/66/8].
1624. Count Mansfeld's expedition. By hd.,
parish and occupation (100) [SP.14/179].
1639. Indenture roll, names only (200)
[SP.16/419].

Shropshire Record Office, Shrewsbury.

Muster Rolls
1579 (published), **1580, 1587, 1588.**
Shrewsbury Town and Liberties (1,500 in
each) [3365/2545-46, 2551-52].
1635. Shrewsbury Town and Liberties
(1,000) [3365/2568].
**1643, 1645. Shrewsbury Town and
Liberties** (500) [3365/2571].

Payments to named soldiers
1522, 1547, 1548, 1596 and n.d.
Shrewsbury Town and Liberties. Incl. men
furnished by the town trade Guilds (50 per
year) [3365/2540].
1590-96. As above (1,500) [3365/2557].

Lists of trained soldiers
**1617, 1618, 1620, 1622. Shrewsbury
Town and Liberties** (50 per year)
[3365/2563].e

SOMERSET

Publications

Muster Certificates: **1569. Whole County** (6,000 names) [P.R.O. SP.12/55] in *Certificates of Musters in the County of Somerset...1569*, ed. Emanuel Green, Somerset Record Soc. **20** (1904).

Trained Bands: **1586.** Four trained bands (300 names each, by hd. only, two at Bridgwater) [P.R.O. SP.12/194] in *Somerset and the Armada*, by E. Green (1888), pp.73-100.

Public Record Office, *Chancery Lane.*

Muster Rolls

1539. Hd. of Stone and Catsash (600) [E.101/59/21], 16 paper ss.; **Hds. of Kingsbury** (385), **South Petherton** (393), **Abdick and Bulston** (708), **Crewkerne** (320) [E.101/59/22], 44 paper ss. See *L&P* **14**, Pt. 1, pp.288-9.

1569. County (6,000) [SP.12/55]. Published.

1572. Hds. of Frome (45), **Wells** (24), **Welford** (44), **Chew** (40), **Keynsham** (45), **Chewton** (20), 5 odd liberties (14 in all) [SP.12/89]. Hd. and names only.

1586. Four bands with 300 names each, by hd. only (Sir Henry Barkley's; Sir Geo. Sydenham's and Sir John Stawell's, both at Bridgwater; Sir John Clyfton's) [SP.12/194]. Published.

1597-1601. Six indenture rolls, 5 by hd., name and parish; 1 by parish and name (from 60 to 300 per roll) [E.101/66/9].

1624. Count Mansfeld's expedition. By hd. and parish (200); by parish and occupation (10); by hd., parish and occupation (100) [SP.14/178].

1626-7. Two indenture rolls (100 each, by parish, occupation) [SP.16/46].

1640. Indenture roll: **Bristol**, by ward and name (200) [SP.16/462].

The British Library Manuscripts Collections.

Muster Rolls

1639. Col. Sir R. Hopton's Band of 200 Foot. By name and parish within hds. [Add.Mss. 28273 f.105]. Also men and weapons to be provided by the Clergy of the deaneries of **Frome** and **Bedminster**. Contains a list of parishes in the two deaneries with the name of the clergyman, the arms (usually a musket) and the name of the man to serve (65 names) [f.115].

Somerset Record Office, *Taunton.*

Muster Rolls, etc.

***c.*1640. Williton and Freemanners Hd.,** trained bands (420) [DD/WO 56/6].

1660. Trained foot soldiers (14 only) from **Axbridge**, tithings of Banwell, Christon, West Street [D/P/ban/23/7].

***c.*1690. Carhampton Hd.,** trained band (86) [DD/DR 53/1-5].

1716. Wells Troop, Somerset Militia. Landowners liable to provide horses, in Hds. of Bruton, Catsash, Chewton, Glaston, Mells and Leigh, Whitleigh, Whitestone, Horethorne, Norton Ferrers and Wells (156 names) [DD/SH 397].

STAFFORDSHIRE

Publications

Muster Rolls: **1539. County: Offlow Hd.** [P.R.O. SP.2/S ff.158-175] in 'The Muster Roll of Staffordshire...1539 (Offlow Hundred)', tr. W. Boyd, *Collections for a History of Staffordshire*, William Salt Archaeological Soc., New Series **4** (1901), pp.215-57; **Cuttlestone** and **Pirehill Hds.** [ff.79-135] **5** (1902), pp.235-324; **Seisdon** and **Totmonslow Hds.** [E.109/59/23] **6**, pt. 1 (1903), pp.63-87. All indexed.

1640. County. (676 names) [Original MS at Wrottesley? Probably augments P.R.O. SP.16/462] in *Collections for a History of Staffs.*, W.S.A.S. 1st Series **15** (1894), p.208. Not indexed.

1685. Pirehill Hd. (127 names) [Chetwynd Papers. Salt Library MSS. Shaw's Collection B28] in Staffordshire Record Soc. **1941** (1942), pp.117-24.

Staffordshire continued

Public Record Office, Chancery Lane.

Muster Rolls
Temp. H.VIII. P. of Hamstall Ridware
(40-50) [E.101/549/20]. 1 paper s. Poor.
Temp. H.VIII. Probably **Offlow Hd.** (200)
[E.101/62/4]. 4m. Poor.
Temp. H.VIII. Offlow Hd. (2,500)
[E.36/18].
1535-6. Cuttlestone Hd. (500-600)
[E.101/58/30]. 27m.
1539. Hds. of Cuttlestone (1,134), Pirehill
(1,084, 1,561) [SP.2/S ff.79-135], written
on both sides but attached in volume at top
so that reverse side is upside down; 'within
county' (820; names only) [SP.2/S
ff.137-56]; **Offlow Hd.** (1,222) [SP.2/S
ff.158-75]; no heading, 6 lists of names
(767) [SP.2/S ff.176-85]. **Seisdon Hd.**
(and Totmanslow Hd.?) (567)
[E.101/59/23]. 4m. All published. See also
L&P **14**, Pt. 1, pp.289-92.
1569. Hds. of Cuttlestone and Seisdon
(940; by hd. only) [SP.12/65]; Hds. of
Offlow (2,000; 29 loose ss.), **Pirehill**
(1,600-700; 21 loose ss,), **City of Lichfield**
(150) [SP.12/56].
1597-1601. Four indenture rolls (3 by hd.,
parish and name; 1 by name only; from 20
to 100 per roll) [E.101/66/11].
1640. Indenture roll, by hd. and name
(300-400) [SP.16/462]. Augments that
published from Wrottesley MSS.

The British Library Manuscripts Collections.

Muster Rolls
1583. Visitation of County (66 names with
hd. and parish): Pirehill (19), Offlow (5),
Seisdon (5), Cuttlestone (7), Totmanslow
(20) [Harl. MSS. 1429].
1590. Names and furniture raised in Staffs.
for Irish service (200 billmen and pikemen)
[Lansd.65]. 13 ms. in poor condition and
very muddled.

Staffordshire Record Office, Stafford.

Muster Roll
1569. Yoxall parish (50) [MS copy made
c.1800].

SUFFOLK

Publications
Military Survey: 1522. Babergh Hd. (2,000
names, by parish, with occupation) [Lincoln
Archives Office, ANC 16/2; transcription of
same at Ipswich Library on which this
publication is based] in *Military Survey of
1522*, Suffolk Record Soc. **28** (1986).
Valuation followed by a section of able men
without substance.
Muster Rolls: 1534-40. As 'Muster-rolls of
the territorials in Tudor times', E. Powell, in
*Proceedings of the Suffolk Institute of
Archaeology* **15**, **16** (1915-27): 1535-6.
Hds. of Blackbourn (Blackford) (360) (**15**,
pp.116-33), **Lothingland and Mutford**
(330) (**16**, pp.36-43) [both P.R.O.
E.101/59/4]; **Lackford** (400) (**15**,
pp.133-43) [E.101/549/9]; **1539.**
Risbridge (340) (**15**, pp.238-52)
[E.101/59/24]; Wilford (457) (**16**,
pp.90-97) [E.36/28 f.30]; **Cosford** (540)
(**16**, pp.211-18) [SP.1/145 ff.108-15];
Half-Hd. of Lothingland (**19**, pp.52-71)
[?date and PRO ref.].
Musters: 1579. Babergh Hd. (part) in
P.S.I.A. **19**, pp.213-26; 1584. **Blackbourn
Hd.** in *P.S.I.A.* **18**, pp.180-210 (together
1,000-1,200 names by parish headed by
constable's name) [both from British Library
Harl. MSS. 366].
Muster Roll: 1631. Hds. of **Hoxon** and
Plomesgate (200 footmen, under Sir
Thomas Glemham), tr. H.W.B. Wayman, in
the *East Anglian, or, Notes and Queries.*
New Series **13** (1909-10), pp.132-5,
150-1, 163-4.
Muster Roll: 1638. County (24,000 names)
[P.R.O. SP.16/411] in *Able Men of Suffolk
1638*, ed. C.E. Banks, Anglo-American
Record Foundation (1931). Indexes of
names and parishes.

Public Record Office, Chancery Lane.

Muster Rolls
1523. Blofield Hd. (114) [SP.1/234 f.31].
Valuation followed by able men. See *L&P
Addenda* 1509-47, Pt. 1, pp.131-2.
1536. Hds. of Blackbourn, Lothingland and
Mutford [E.101/59/4], **Lackford**
[E.101/549/9]. Published.
1539. Hds. of Risbridge [E.101/59/24],
Wilford [E.36/28 f.30], Cosford [SP.1/145
ff.108-15]. Published. See also *L&P* **14**, Pt.
1, pp.292-3.

Suffolk: *P.R.O.*: *Muster Rolls* continued

1539. Hds. of **Loes, Woodbridge** [SP.1/145 ff.99-107], poor, very mutilated; **Thredling** (150) [SP.2/S ff.186-7]. See *L&P* **14**, Pt. 1, pp. 292-3.

1584. Lowestoft Town (250), **Lothingland Half-Hd.** (450) [SP.12/167].

1590-1601. Four indenture rolls, by hd., name and parish (from 25 to 200 per roll) [E.101/66/12].

1624. Count Mansfeld's expedition. By parish (100); names only (300) [SP.14/179].

1631. Blything Hd. (170; 'Capt. Bruster's Band') [SP.16/199]; **Lackford Hd.** (350) [SP.16/201]. Both by parish and name.

1638. County (24,000) [SP.16/411]. Published.

The British Library Manuscripts Collections.

Muster Rolls

1577. Blackbourn or **Blackford Hd.**: 55 trained shotte by parish; 145 pikemen, bowmen, billmen [Harl. MSS. 309]; **Whole County** in lists (2,500-2,700) [f.219], 7 double sided closely written; mutilated, fading and difficult; much struck out, possibly a draft.

1584. Blackbourn (Blackford) **Hd.** (1,000-200) [Harl. MSS. 366]. Published.

Lincoln Archives Office, Lincoln.

Muster Roll

1522. Babergh Hd. (2,000) [ANC 16/2; transcript at Ipswich Library]. Published.

Suffolk Record Office, Bury St. Edmunds.

Muster Roll

1635. Bury St. Edmunds Borough (1,400 able men aged 16-60, by ward) [D I.2/1; also TS. of a transcript by Peter Christie, 1973, indexed; B 45.5].

SURREY

Publications

Muster Rolls: **County** (more western half than eastern): **1544-1684** [Surrey R.O., Guildford, LM 1330], in *Surrey Musters*, tr. T. Craib, Surrey Record Soc. 3 (originally numbered 2, 10, 11; 13: index) (1914-19): **2:** 1544, 1569, 1583-4; **10:** 1569, 1572-4, 1584-5, 1588, 1592-3, 1596; **11:** 1596, n.d. (temp. Eliz.), 1642, 1670-2, 1675-6, 1684. Useful summary of years and hds.

Surrey continued

Public Record Office, Chancery Lane.

Muster Rolls

1539. Hds. of **Blackheath** (252), **Tandridge** (375), **Reigate** (390), **Wotton** (300) [E.36/24 f.2]; **Wallington** (623) [E.36/24 f.32]. See *L&P* **14**, Pt. 1, pp.294-5.

1548. Hds. of **Tandridge** (240), **Reigate** (170) [SP.10/3/16]. Calendar says 'whole county', heading also says Hd. of Copthorne and Effingham, and Hd. of Kingston and Elmbridge, but not found.

1569. Hds. of **Brixton** (240), **Woking** (600-50), **Godalming** (300), **Godley** (230), **Farnham** (275), **Blackheath and Wotton** (620); **Kingston and Elmbridge** (350), **Copthorne and Effingham** (270), **Tandridge** (220), **Reigate** (250), **Wallington** (summary of nos. only) [SP.12/5]. Published edition of *Surrey Musters* augments this.

1569 (also). **Hds.** of **Blackheath and Wotton** (850-900), **Godalming** (550-600), **Farnham** (350-400), **Woking** (750-800), **Godley** (450-500), **Kingston and Elmbridge** (600-50), **Copthorne and Effingham** (550-600), **Reigate and Tandridge** (1,400-1,500), **Brixton and Wallington** (1,700-1,800) [SP.12/50].

1600-01. Two indenture rolls, by parish and name (15 entries per roll) [E.101/66/13].

1624. Count Mansfeld's expedition. By occupation (50); names only (200) [SP.14/179].

The British Library Manuscripts Collections.

Muster Roll

1627. 'A Muster of 100 footmen for the Low Countries'. Name and parish of 70 men; rest lost by mutilation [Add. MSS. 290609B].

Surrey Record Office, Guildford.

Muster Rolls

1544, 1569, 1572-74, 1583-84, 1587, 1588, 1592-93, 1596, 1597, 1642, 1670-73, 1675 or 1767, 1684. County [LM 1330]. Published.

Greater London Record Office, 40 Northampton Road, EC1R OHB.

Militia Book

1660. Southwark Militia Book. p.8r. [rnp/P92/SAV/525].

SUSSEX

Public Record Office, Chancery Lane.

Muster Rolls
Temp. H.VIII. Area unknown
[E.101/549/21]. 52 fragmented pages,
readable in places but difficult to identify.
1539. Rape of Bramber (also Fishergate):
Duchess of Norfolk's parks (20),
Singlecross Hd. (140), Horsham Borough
(50), Hds. of West Grinstead (55),
Windham (30), Street (30), Fishergate
(30), Shoreham Town (20) [E.36/45].
1539 also. **Rape of Arundel:** Hds. of
Rotherbridge (508), Easwrith (684)
[E.36/45]. See *L&P* **14**, Pt. 1, pp.296-7.
1539 also. **Rape of Hastings:** Hds. of
Hawksborough (234), Shoywell (146),
Henhurst (89), Ninfield (99), Robertsbridge
(58), Bexhill (67), Netherfield (82), Foxearle
(128), Battle (120), Staple (142), Goldspur
(169), Guestling (89), Baldslow (133),
Gostrow (94) [E.36/50]. See *L&P* **14**, Pt.
1, p.298.
1539 also. **City of Chichester** (320) [SP.2/S
ff.188-200]. See *L&P* **14**, Pt. 1, p.295.
1539 also. **Rape of Chichester:** Servants of
the Earls of Arundel and Southampton, and
Lord Lawarr (363), Hds. of Easebourne
(367), Dumpford (236), Westbourne and
Singleton (350), Bosham (194) [SP.2/S
ff.201-24], Box (133), Stockbridge (111),
Manhood (173), Aldwick (115) [ff.226-34].
L&P **14**, Pt. 1. pp.295-6.
1539 also. **Rape of Arundel:** Avisford Hd.
(265), Arundel Borough (69), Poling Hd.
(382) [SP.2/S ff.236-46]. See *L&P* **14**, Pt.
1, p.296.
1539 also. **Rape of Bramber:** Brightford Hd.
(225), Steyning Borough and Hd. (161),
East Easwrith Hd. (68) [SP.2/S ff.251-59].
See *L&P* **14**, Pt. 1, p.297.
1539 also. **Rape of Pevensey:** Hd. of
Longbridge (126), East Grinstead (90),
Hartfield (122), Loxfield (622), Rotherfield
(171), Totmore (85), Flexborough (51), Dill
(83), Rushmonden (260), Alciston (69),
Willingdon (80), Eastbourne (82), Shiplake
(147), Perkgate (6) [SP.2/S ff.260-94]. See
L&P **14**, Pt. 1, pp.298-9.
1548. Rapes of Bramber (100), **Chichester**
(100) [SP.10//3/17,18]. Within hds. only.
1569. Rapes of Bramber, Lewes, Arundel
(100 each, names by hd. only), **City and
Rape of Chichester** (600) [SP.12/6].

P.R.O.: Muster Rolls continued

1597. Indenture roll (25) [E.101/66/14].
1624. Count Mansfeld's expedition. By hd.
(50) [SP.14/179].

The British Library Manuscripts Collections.

Muster Roll
1583. Names of Gentlemen furnishing out
horses and lances within the Rapes of
Chichester (31), Arundel (37), Bramber
(24), Lewes (40), Pevensey (58) and
Hastings (35) (sometimes after name, 'of
... parish') [Harl. MSS. 703].

East Sussex Record Office, *Lewes.*

Muster Rolls
1619. Hds. of **Staple, Henhurst,
Hawksborough, Robertsbridge,
Netherfield** and **Battle** (160, divided into
'dry pikes', corslets and muskets) [Dunn of
Stonehouse in Warbleton 52/6/1].
*c.*1625-*c.*1630. Hds. of **Hawksborough,
Foxearle, Bexhill** (100-150 each)
[52/6/2-4].

West Sussex Record Office, *Chichester.*

Muster Rolls
1620-21. Rape of Arundel, Avisford Hd.:
parish returns for Barnham, Binsted,
Eastergate, Felpham and Bilsham, Ford,
Climping and Atherington, Madehurst,
Middleton and Elmer, South Stoke and
Offham, Tortington, Walberton, and
Yapton; **Bury Hd.:** Ashford and Hurst in
Wisborough Green, Bury and West Burton,
Coldwaltham and Watersfield, Houghton,
and Sand in Fittleworth; **Rape of Lewes,
Swanborough Hd.** (180) [Add. Ms. 2741].

Note. It is understood that there are many
Sussex muster returns for the 1660's in the
archive of the Duke of Northumberland at
Alnwick Castle, a period when the Duke
was Lord Lieutenant.

WARWICKSHIRE

Publication
Muster Rolls: **1599. Hds.** of **Barlichway** and
Kineton. Three divisions of the Trained
Band, described as 'Mr. Cooke's' (35),
'Mr. Kempson's' (50), and 'Mr. Williams''
(186) [transcribed from the original return
in the possession of the Earl of Warwick,
'which itself was a draft from which it was
prepared'], in *The Muster Rolls for the
Hundreds of Barlichway and
Kineton...1599*, by the Revd. J.H. Bloom,
Rector of Whitchurch, 1905.
See also under Shakespeare Birthplace Trust
Record Office.

Public Record Office, *Chancery Lane.*

Muster Rolls
Temp. H.VIII. Barlichway Hd. (1,000 +)
[E.101/62/5]. 10m.
1523. Kington Hd. (parishes of Cherington
and Honington only) (78) [SP.1/234 f.37].
See *L&P Addenda 1509-47*, Pt.1, p.132.
1569. Hds. of **Kington** (500), **Hemlingford**
(670; incl. Birmingham: 70), **Knightlow**
(525), **City of Coventry** (250) [SP.12/61].
1569 also. **Hds.** of **Hemlingford** (700-50),
Knightlow (500-50), **City of Coventry**
(250), **Hds.** of **Barlichway** (400-50),
Kington (500-50) [SP.12/65]. Some lost at
page ends.
1590-1600. Five indenture rolls: 4 by hd.
and parish (from 60 to 300 per roll); 1 by
hd. only (120) [E.101.66/55].
1605. Barlichway Hd. (125) [SP.12/61;
with 1569 roll above].
·**1624.** Count Mansfeld's expedition. Three
lists (by parish and occupation: 200, 400,
50) [SP.14/178].

Warwickshire County Record Office, *Warwick.*

Muster Rolls or Military Surveys
1522. Knightlow Hd. (67 places; list
available at W.C.R.O.). Lists male
inhabitants over 16, by parish or hamlet
[HR 65/1]. See also under Coventry City
R.O.
1577, 1580. Horsemen (lances and light
horse), provided by named Warw.
gentlemen, arranged by hd. [HR.65/3/1-5].
1660. The following items are incl. in a book
entitled 'Muster of the County of Warwick
1660 MS', now in the Beinecke Rare Book
and Manuscript Library, Yale University

Warwickshire C.R.O.: *Muster Rolls* contd.
Library, of which there is a microfilm at
W.C.R.O. [MI.378].
County. Horse and Foot. List of trained
soldiers by hd. and parish [f.10r].
Hd. of **Knightlow** and **Hemlingford**...and
City of Coventry (names by parish) [f.34r].
Hds. of **Kineton** and **Barlichway.** List of
horse [f.38r.].
Coventry. Lists of foot arms [f.56r, 59r].

'Militia Book'
1659. County and Coventry [microfilm M.1
229, of original in possession of the Earl of
Aylesford, Packington Hall, Warw.],
comprising **Knightlow** and **Hemlingford**
Hds. (names) [f.3], **Kineton Hd.** (names)
[f.7]; horse and arms: 3 separate returns
supplementing each other, covering
different places in the same hds. (names)
[f.10]; **Coventry** (individual persons)
[ff.23]. There are other lists, but not
apparently naming invididuals.

Coventry City Record Office.

Muster Certificates, Rolls etc.
1522. County of the City of Coventry and
surrounding hamlets (1,000) [Acc. 24/1].
Arranged by ward and village, plus priests
and outsiders.
1624-40. Coventry. Musters of trained men,
by ward and village (300) [Corpn. Admin.
Records: 17c. Defence: W.550, 984, 987
(/2, 3, 8-10), 1699].
1640. Coventry. Impressed soldiers (43)
[C.A.R.: 17c. Defence: W.990/5].
*c.***1640. Coventry.** Muster of trained men,
by ward, village and Clothiers' Company
(56) [C.A.R.: 17c. Defence W.1428
(part)].
*c.***1641. Coventry.** Lists (2 each) of men
and women required to provide arms or
arm themselves, and of trained men, by
wards and villages (42) [C.A.R: 17c.
Defence: W.964].

Shakespeare Birthplace Trust Record Office, *Stratford upon Avon.*

Muster Rolls
1536-7. Stratford on Avon. Able men (also
incl. Old Stratford, Snitterfield, Sherborne,
Shottery) [printed, but 10 copies only].
1669. County. Those supplying horses only
(150) [ER 10/8/1].

WESTMORLAND

Publication
1539. County. 'Names of all the Gentlemen
within the Shire...' (65) [British Library,
Cotton MSS. Calig. B.III, f.192], in
*Calendar of State Papers: Letters and
Papers H.VIII*, **14**, Pt.2, pp.319-20.

Public Record Office, Chancery Lane.

Muster Rolls
1627. Indenture roll: **West** and **Middle Ward**
(10), **East Ward** (15) [SP.16/72].

The British Library Manuscripts Collections.

1539. County. 'Gentlemen within the
Shire...' (65) [Cotton MSS. Calig. B.III,
f.192]. Published.

Cumbria Record Office, Carlisle.

Muster Roll
1715. Kirkby Lonsdale Ward
[D/Lons/L.13/6/22].

WILTSHIRE

Publication
Muster Rolls. **1539. North Wiltshire** [P.R.O.
E.36/46]. Published by Sir Thomas Phillipps
1834 [from the original then in the Chapter
House, Westminster]. The only known
copies of this rare publication are in the
British Library (North Room) and the
Wiltshire Record Office.

Public Record Office, Chancery Lane.

Muster Rolls
1535. City of New Sarum: Market Ward
(130), **Martin Ward** (75), **New Street Ward**
(105), **Mede Ward** (40) [E.101/549/3]. 9
paper ss. Marked 'Cantab. Money'.
1539. Hds. of Melksham (109), **Bradford**
(93), **Warminster** (156), **Westbury** (73),
Liberty of Trowbridge (77) [SP.1/145
ff.117-22]; **Hds. of Alderbury** (186), **Chalk**
(211), **Frustfield** (52), **Underditch** (74),
Downton (164), **South Damerton** (130),
Cawdon and Cadworth (250) [ff.125-34];
City of New Sarum (733) [ff.136-41];
Hds. of Amesbury (220), **Swanborough**
(480), **Potterne and Cannings** (291),
Elstub and Everley (238) [ff.143-55]. See
L&P **14**, Pt. 1, pp.299-301.

Wiltshire: *P.R.O.: Muster Rolls* contd.

1539 also. **Hds. of Kinwardstone** (277),
Kingsbridge (273), **Selkley** (329),
Ramsbury (156), **Highworth, Cricklade
and Staple** (86) [EP.36/46 f.3]; **North
Damerham** (102), **Chippenham** (529),
Calne (163), **Whorwelsdown** (192),
Malmesbury (301) [E.36/46 f.33].
Published (British Library and Wilts. R.O.
only). See also *L&P* **14**, Pt. 1, pp.302-3;
21, Pt. 2, pp.205-6; Wilts. Archaeological
& Nat. Hist. Soc. **7** (1862).
1559. City of New Sarum (550-600, by
wards) [SP.12/2].
1590-1601. Nine indenture rolls (5 by army
division and parish; 4 by parish; from 30 to
300 per roll) [E.101/66/16].
1624. Count Mansfeld's expedition. Two
lists, by parish and occupation (200, 250)
[SP.14/178]; by hd. and occupation (100)
[SP.14/179].

Wiltshire Record Office, *Trowbridge.*

Muster Rolls
1539. North Wilts. Published copy.
1601. Marlborough. Men for armour
(70-80) [Marlborough Borough Records.
G.22/1/107].
1660. Hd. of Kingsbridge and Selkley.
Capt. Calley's Company, named men to
serve as corsleteers or musketeers [Calley
family papers 1178/448]; List of
landowners required to provide militia
service [1178/450].
1670-74. Salisbury. Trained Band list
[Salisbury City Records].
1685. Salisbury area (Hds. of Alderbury,
Chalke, Swanborow, Amesbury, Elstubb
and Everly, Cawdon and Cadworth,
Underditch, Downton, Frustfield, Branch
and Dole) (540, by hd. and parish)
[490/1410].
1715. South-west Wilts. People to provide
men, *or* men enrolled (200) [413/12].

WORCESTERSHIRE

Public Record Office, Chancery Lane.

Muster Rolls

Temp. H.VIII. Hds. of Halfshire, Oswaldslow, Droitwich (2,500) [E.36/35]. Book of 130pp.

Temp. H.VIII. Hds. of Halfshire, Oswaldslow (1,000-1,200) [E.36/36]. Book of 60pp.

1535. Pershore Hd. (700-800) [E.101/58/28]. 10m. Damaged in parts.

1536. City of Worcester [E.101/62/7]. 8m. Scrappy, almost unreadable.

1539. City of Worcester (445; by ward) [E.101/59/25]. 6m. Mostly useless, badly faded. See *L&P* **14**, Pt. 1, p.303.

1539 also. Parts of **Oswaldslow** (24) [SP.1/145 f.160], 2m., bad; **Doddingtree** (66) [f.161], 2m., bad; unknown [f.162], useless. See *L&P* **14**, Pt. 1, p.305.

1539 also. **Hds. of Blackenhurst** (345) [E.36/27 f.1]; **Oswaldslow** (970) [f.21] (numbers differ from calendar by several hundred; some ss. missing?); **Halfshire** (600-700) [f.53] (less mutilated than calendar suggests; well repaired). See *L&P* **14**, Pt. 1, pp.303-6.

1542. City and Liberty of Worcester (815). 2m. Faded and difficult. See *L&P* **17**, p.510.

1597-1601. Ten indenture rolls (6 with names only; 2 with hds., parishes and names; 2 with parishes and names; from 30 and 100 per roll) [E.101/66/7].

1624. Count Mansfeld's expedition. Two lists, names only (100 each) [SP.14/179].

1639. Indenture roll (230; by parish and name) [SP.16/419].

1640. Indenture roll (600; by band, hd. and name) [SP.16/462].

Hereford and Worcester Record Office, St Helen's, Fish Street, Worcester.

Muster Rolls

1640s (the document is dated '164-'). **County** (1,000) [705:93 BA 845/5].

YORK and the AINSTY

Public Record Office, Chancery Lane.

Muster Rolls

1539. City of York, by wards: Bootham (429), Monk (233), Walmgate (437), Micklegate and North Street (286), Ainsty (397), further of Ainsty (404) [E.36/32]. See L&P **14**, Pt. 1, pp.306-7.

1539 also. **Liberty of St. Mary's Abbey** (350) [SP.1/145 ff.164-7].

1548. City of York and **Wapentake of the Ainsty,** by wards (1,000 +) [SP.10/3/10].

1597-1601. York City and West Riding: one indenture roll [E.101.66/18].

1640. York City, by wards and names. Indenture roll (12) [SP.16/462].

City of York Archives Department.

Note. Unless otherwise stated the lists cover the City of York and the Wapentake of the Ainsty.

Muster Rolls

Note. Whilst the 16th century lists have proved useful, since they list weapons owned and give indications of status, they are not easy to use, and may take inordinate time to come up with a single name (a clear case for transcription and indexing. *Ed.*).

1539, 1542 (2,000) [E.64].

1543 (1,000) [E.41].

1573 (1,500) [E47].

1584, 1587 (3,000) [E.41a].

1666. Ainsty only (pt.) (200) [E.47a].

1745. 'The Association' volunteers [E.130].

YORKSHIRE: EAST RIDING

Publications

Muster Roll: **1584. East Riding:** Wapentakes of Dickering, Harthill, Holderness, Howdenshire, Ouse and Derwent, Kingston-upon-Hull, Town and Liberties of Beverley, in *Miscellanea* **5**, Yorkshire Archaeological Soc. Record Series **115** (1951), p.69. Mostly as to Arms. Name index.

Muster Roll: **1625. Wapentake of Buckrose** (57 names) [MSS Hull Museum], in East Riding Antiquarian and N.H. Society **21** (1915), pp.1-6.

Public Record Office, Chancery Lane.

Muster Rolls
1539. Wapentake of Buckrose (724),
Liberty of Howden (511), **Wapentakes** of
Ouse and Derwent (950), **Dickering**
(1,184), **Holderness (South Balery)** (216),
(North Balery) (941) [E.36/30] (Holderness
very difficult indeed); **Wapentake of**
Harthill (3,000+) [E.36/39]. See *L&P* **14**,
Pt. 1, pp.307-10.
1539 also. **Kingston upon Hull** (250; by
wards), **'Super Hull'** (200) [E.101/60/1].
1595. Wapentakes of Dickering and
Buckrose (18 horsemen only), **Harthill**
(400), **Town of Beverley** (20),
Wapentakes of Ouse and Derwent (160),
Howdenshire (160) [SP.12/256].
1597-1601. Two indenture rolls (from 80 to
100 per roll); two rolls for all Ridings (200
each) [E.101/66/18].
1640. Indenture roll (45) [SP.16/462].

Kingston upon Hull City Record Office.

Muster Rolls
1538. Kingston upon Hull Town (*i.e.* within
the walls) only [CAM 1-5].
1599. Town and County (of Kingston upon
Hull) [CAM 6].
1667. Town only, incomplete [CAM 7-9].

The Borthwick Institute of Historical
Research, York.

Muster Rolls
1745. Lists of companies of foot soldiers
during the Jacobite rebellion (several
hundred names) [Bp.C&P. XXI].

YORKSHIRE: NORTH RIDING

Publications
1588. 'Men, Money and Arms', in parish of
Wholeton (Whorlton) (65 names); also
extracts from Lame Soldiers and Hospital
Book, *c.*1600; in *North Riding Quarter*
Sessions Records, Pt. 2, North Riding
Record Soc. **2** (1884).

Public Record Office, Chancery Lane.

Muster Rolls
Temp. H.VIII. Wapentake of Allerton
(400-500) [E.101/549/22]. 9 paper ss.
1535. Wapentake of Rydale (300+)
[E.101/549/4]. 1m.
1535 also. Parishes named from all parts of
Riding (1,000+) [E.101/549/7]. Vastly
faded and confused. Seems to be part of a
larger book; 27pp. removed (numbered
303-358).
1535 also. Area unknown (300)
[E.101/58/29]. 3m. Most difficult.
1535 also. **Hd. of Gilling West** (800), **Hang**
East (500), **Hang West** (1,500),
Wapentakes of Halikeld (250), **Gilling East**
(450) [E.36/44].
1539. Wapentake of Birdforth and Liberty
of Byland and Newburgh (800) [E.36/23
f.1]; **Wapentakes of Hang East** (608) and
Hallikeld (322) [f.25]; **Gilling West** (1,380)
[f.75]; **Pickering** (1,044) [f.119]; **Liberty**
of Allertonshire 342) [E.36/44 f.133]
(?**1535** but 1539 in calendar; fading and
difficult); **Wapentakes of Hang West**
(1,452) [E.36/41 f.1], **Langbargh** (1,455)
[E.36/41 f.53]; **Liberty of Whitby Strand**
(950) [SP.2/S f.296] (difficult hand);
Wapentake of Rydale (1,196) [SP.36/41
f.95]. See *L&P* **14**, Pt. 1, pp.311-5.
1542. Wapentakes of Pickering (1,052),
Borough of Scarborough (108), **Liberty of**
Whitby Strand and Whitby (339),
Lordship of Spawton (74) [SP.1/173
f.188]. See *L&P* **17**, p.510.
1595. Wapentakes of Rydale (200),
Birdforth (175), **Richmondshire**(?) (44)
[SP.12/256].
1597-1601. Two indenture rolls (100 each);
two rolls for all Ridings (200 each)
[E.101/66/18].
1640. Indenture roll (55) [SP.16/462].

The British Library Manuscripts Collections.

Muster Roll
1598-1606. Two companies of 100 men;
names and parishes [Add. MSS. 36293:
Letter Book of Ralph, Lord Eure, ff.10-12].

The Borthwick Institute of Historical
Research, York. •

Muster Rolls
1745. Lists of companies of foot soldiers
during the Jacobite rebellion (several
hundred names) [Bp.C.&P. XXI].

YORKSHIRE: WEST RIDING

Publications
Muster Roll: **1535. Claro Wapentake**
[P.R.O. E.36/37], by W. P. Baildon, in
Miscellanea 5, Thoresby Soc. **15** (1909),
pp.111-21 (marked 'to be continued', but
no further publication).
Muster Roll: **1539. Skyrack Wapentake**
[P.R.O. SP.1/145], by W.P. Baildon, in
Miscellanea 2, Thoresby Soc. **4** (1895),
pp.244-60, and *Miscellanea 3*, Thoresby
Soc. **9** (1899), pp.99-111, 299-310.

Public Record Office, Chancery Lane.

Muster Rolls
Temp. H.VIII. Morley Wapentake (?)
(1,000 +) [E.101/62/9]. 2m.
1524. Retinue of Lord Darcy for the wars
against the Scots, by Lordships
(2,000-2,100; each headed by captain,
petty captain and chaplain) [E.36/43]. Book
of 52pp.
1535. Whole West Riding (?) (5,000)
[E.101/62/8]. 6m.
1535 also. Wapentakes of **Barkston Ash**
(700 +) [E.101/549/5], 20m.; **Skyrack**
(1,600-1,700) [E.101/549/6], 49m.
1535 also. **Claro Wapentake** (750),
Liberties of Knaresborough (Forest and
Soke) (650), **Kirkby Malzeard** (220), **Ripon**
(350) [E.36/37]. Claro Wapentake
published.
1539. Skyrack Wapentake (986) [SP.1/145
ff.171-92]. Published. See also *L&P* **14**, Pt.
1, pp.315-6.
1539 also. Wapentakes of **Osgoldcross**
(1,489) [SP.1/146 ff.1-79]; **Ewcross**
(1,507) [ff.82-109]; **Barkston Ash** (2,100)
[ff.110-39]. See *L&P* **14**, Pt. 1, pp.318-9.
1539 also. **Staincliffe** (Craven) **Wapentake**
(2,610), **Forest of Bowland** (503),
servants of Sir Thomas Tempest and John
Lambart (28) [E.36/34]. See *L&P* **14**, Pt. 1,
pp.317-8.
1539 also. **Claro Wapentake** and **Liberty of
Knaresborough Forest** (1,250) [E.36/37
f.97]. See *L&P* **14**, Pt. 1, pp.316-7.

P.R.O.: Muster Rolls continued
1539 also. **Liberty of Bradford** and
household of Dame Tempest (538)
[E.36/38 f.1]. See *L&P* **14**, Pt. 1, p.319.
1539 also. **Liberty of Ripon** (587) [E.36/38
f.17]. See *L&P* **14**, Pt. 1, p.315.
1539 also. **Liberty and Soke of
Knaresborough** (404) [E.36/38 f.31]. See
L&P **14**, Pt. 1, p.317.
1539 also. **Liberty of Kirkby Malzeard** (355)
[E.36/38 f.49]. See *L&P* **14**, Pt. 1, p.315.
1595. Wapentakes of Agbrigg and Morley
(400), **Strafforth and Tickhill** (300,
alphabetical by parish), **Barkston Ash**
(200) [SP.12/256].
1597-1601. Five indenture rolls (from 80 to
100 per roll); one roll with York City; two
all Ridings (200) [E.101/62/18].
1626-7. Wakefield and adjoining wapentake,
indenture roll (67, by parish) [SP.16/46].
1640. Indenture roll (88) [SP.16/462].

The British Library Manuscripts Collections.
Muster Rolls
1633. Major Reresby's Company (120
names by parish) [Add. MSS. Ch.54396].
1660. Wapentakes of **Strafforth and
Tickhill** (77 townships, 500-600 names)
[Add. MSS. 28082, ff.14-24]; **Osgoldcross**
(50 townships, 450-500 names) [ff.26-35].

*Bradford District Archives, 15 Canal Road,
Bradford.*

Muster Rolls
1573-86. Wapentakes of **Osgoldcross,
Staincross, Aggbrigg and Morley** (1,000)
[MM/C/18; transcript only].
17th cent. Skyrack Wapentake (120)
[Sp.St. 10/7/1].

*Kirklees District Archives, Central Library,
Huddersfield.*

Muster Roll
**1638-39. Wapentake of Agbrigg and
Morley.** Capt. Thomas Beaumont's
company in regt. of Sir William Savill (100)
[DD/WBA/6 and 8; transcript only].

WALES and MONMOUTHSHIRE

Public Record Office, Chancery Lane.

Muster Rolls
1595-1601. No counties or other location given. 28 indenture rolls (8: names only; 12: hd. and names; 8: parish and names; varying from 15 to 100 per roll) [E.101/66/19]. Some fragile.

ANGLESEY

Public Record Office, Chancery Lane.

Muster Rolls
1539. Hds. or **Commotes** of **Dindaethwy** (Tyndeathwy) (204), **Menai** (204), **Malltraeth** (151), **Llifion** (148), **Twrcelyn** (171), **Talybolyon** (200), **Towns** of **Beaumaris** (100) and **Newborough** (33) [E.36/33]. Difficult. See *L&P* **14**, Pt. 1, p.321.

National Library of Wales, Aberystwyth.

Muster Rolls
*c.*1534-63. **Menai Hd.** [Llanfair & Brynodol P 489] (possibly a copy of P.R.O. E.36/33].
*c.*1600. **County** [NLW MS 1548.F ff.68-9]. The following records, 1602-49, are all in 'Carreglwyd I':
1602, 1614. Talybolion Hd. [257].
1615. Dindaethwy Hd. [1810].
1616. Talybolion Hd. (trained bands) [167].
1619. Talybolion Hd. (trained bands) [1659]; **Dindaethwy Hd.** (able men 'which do not trayne') [2410], ('who may be called to take up arms') [168], ('as are of ability to bear arms and are not charged with any' [67]; **Llifon Hd.** (trained band) [1811]; Llanfaethlu parish (trained band) [1795].
1622. Talybolion Hd. (to provide horses) [1592].
1625. Dindaethwy Hd. (trained bands) [167].
1644. Talybolion Hd. (trained bands) [1619].
1649. Llifon Hd. [101].

BRECON or BRECKNOCK

Public Record Office, Chancery Lane.

Muster Rolls
1539. Lordship of Brecknock (2,015) [SP.1/146 ff.140-74]. See *L&P* **14**, Pt. 1, p.322.
1539 also. **Lordships of Builth** (820), **Cantref Selyf** (428), **Glynbwch and the Haye** (153) [E.36/20 f.61]. See *L&P* **14**, Pt. 1, p.328.
1542. Lordships of Welsh Talgarth and English Talgarth (430) [SP.1/173 ff.211-12]. A lot lost. See *L&P* **17**, pp.510-1.
1640. Indenture roll (200; by parish and name) [SP.16/462].

The British Library Manuscripts Collections

Muster Rolls, Trained Bands, etc.
Volume headed 'Muster Rolls *etc.* Co. Brecon 1608-37' [Add. MSS. 10609]. Each band 100 men. Comprising:
1615. Parishes of Talgarth and Devynock [ff.5-17], some deletions, heading mutilated; Penkelly and Crickhowell [ff.18-30].
n.d. Gentry and Clergy [f.45].
1620(?). Parishes of Builth and Merthyr Cynog [f.49]. Many deletions. Muddled. Probably several years bound together.
1620. Parishes of Talgarth and Devynock [f.61]; Penkelly and Crickhowell [f.71].
1624. One hundred men for Ireland, parishes of Talgarth, Penkelly, Builth, Merthyr Cynog, borough of Brecon, parishes of Crickhowell, Devynock [f.124].
1637. Parishes of Builth and Merthyr Cynog. [f.89]; Talgarth and Devynock [f.99]; Penkelly and Crickhowell [f.108].
n.d. List of 250 names within parishes of Devynock, Merthyr Cynog, Penkelly, Crickhowell, Talgarth and Brecon (purpose unclear) [ff.118-123].

WALES continued

CAERNARVONSHIRE

Public Record Office, Chancery Lane.

Muster Rolls
1539. Commote of Isgwyrfai (347); **Town of Caernarvon** (92), **Commotes of Uwchgwyrfai** (213), **Uchaf** (200), **Gwynedd** (407), **Isaf** (318), **Nantconway** (200), **Dinllaen**(160), **Cafflogion** (170), **Cymydmaen** (254) [E.36/49 f.1]. See *L&P* **14**, Pt. 1, p.324.
1640. Indenture roll (150) [SP.16/462].

National Library of Wales, Aberystwyth.

Muster Book
1639. County: trained bands [Llanfair & Brynodol P 499].

CARDIGANSHIRE

Public Record Office, Chancery Lane.

Muster Rolls
1640. Indenture roll (150) [SP.16/6462].

CARMARTHENSHIRE

Public Record Office, Chancery Lane.

Muster Rolls
1539. Commotes of Is Cennen (144), **Carnwyllion** (84), **Lordship of Cloigin**(?) (38), tenants of Ric. More (33), **Commote of Cedweli** (30) [SP.2/S ff.311-15]. See *L&P* **14**, Pt. 1, p.322.
1539 also. Lordships of **Llanymddyfri** (Llandovery) (703), **Llansadurn** (123), **Laugharne** (290), **Emlyn** (256) [SP.2/S ff.316-41]. See *L&P* **14**, Pt. 1, pp.323-4.
1539 also. **Kidwelly Hd.** (incl. Llanelli) [E.36/42 f.9]. See *L&P* **14**, Pt. 1, p.327.

DENBIGHSHIRE

Public Record Office, Chancery Lane.

Muster Rolls
1539. Lordships of Bromfield, Yale and **Chirk** (1,544) [E.36/49 f.63] 39pp. See *L&P* **14**, Pt. 1, p.322.
1539 also. **Commote of Ceinmeirch** (333), **Is Dulas** (352), **Uwch Aled** (268), **Uwch Dulas** (402), **Denbigh Town** (196), **Is Aled Commote** (463) [E.36/20 f.1]. See *L&P* **14**, Pt. 1, p.325.
1539 also. **Lordships of Cynllaith-Owen** and **Stanage** (Rad.) (100) [E.36/20 f.54]. See *L&P* **14**, Pt. 1, p.327.
1539 also. **Town and Lordship of Ruthin** (626) [SP.1/146 ff.221-31]. See *L&P* **14**, Pt. 1, pp.328.
1639. Indenture roll (150; by hd. and name) [SP.161/419].
1640. Indenture roll (180; by division and name) [SP.16/462].

FLINTSHIRE

Public Record Office, Chancery Lane.

Muster Rolls
1539. County (2,295; by parish) [SP.1/146 ff.179-219]. Mostly good. See *L&P* **14**, Pt. 1, pp.325-6.
1539 also. **Lordships of Hawarden** (256), **Mohuntesdale** (Moldsdale) (337) [E.36/49 f.52]. 22pp. See *L&P* **14**, Pt. 1, p.326.
1639. Indenture roll (70; by hd. and name) [SP.16/419].

GLAMORGAN

Public Record Office, Chancery Lane.

Muster Rolls
1539. Llandaff Lordship (118, by parish) [SP.2/S ff.350-1; Sir Rice Mansell's servants and tenants in Glamorgan and Gower (235) [ff.351-3]. See *L&P* **14**, Pt. 1, p.326.
1548-9. Llantrisant Hd. (120) [SP.10/4/1].
1639. Indenture roll (150; by hd., parish and name) [SP.16/419].
1640. Indenture roll (200; by hd., parish and name) [SP.16/462].

WALES continued

MERIONETH

Public Record Office, Chancery Lane

Muster Rolls
1539. Hds. or **Commotes of Ystumanner** (299), Ardudwy (646; incl. 25 from Hardelegh (Harlech?)), **Talbont** (400), **Penllyn** (319), **Edeyrnion** (222) [E.36/33]. Hard. See *L&P* **14**, Pt. 1, pp.321-2.

1539 also. **Lordship of Mowthou** (Mawddwy) (50) [E.36/49f.50]. See *L&P* **14**, Pt. 1, p.327.

National Library of Wales, Aberystwyth.

Muster Rolls [Peniarth MS. 431.E].
Early 17th cent. Commote of Ardudwy Uwch Artro.
Early 17th cent. Edeyrnion Hd. (men bearing unserviceable arms and men not charged).
1608. Hds. of Penllyn and Edeyrnion.
1644. Talybont Uwch Cregennan: list of soldiers.

MONMOUTHSHIRE
(administratively in England until 1974)

Public Record Office, Chancery Lane.

Muster Rolls
1539. Abergavenny (1,100) [E.36/26 f.1]. See *L&P* **14**, Pt. 1, p.321.
1539 also. **Newport Town** (109); **Wentloog Hd.**(516) [E.36/42 f.9]. 37pp. See *L&P* **14**, Pt. 1, p.327.
1539 also. **Lordships of Usk, Caerleon, Trelleck** (1,108) [E.36/26 f.22]. Difficult and confused. See *L&P* **14**, Pt. 1, pp.329.
1600-01. Five indenture rolls (by hd., name and parish, varying between 25 and 100 per roll) [E.101/66/3].
1639. Indenture roll (115; by hd., parish and name) [SP.16/419].

MONTGOMERYSHIRE

Public Record Office, Chancery Lane.

Muster Rolls
1539. Deuddwr and Welshpool (337) [E.101/59/26]. Repaired, but very faded. See *L&P* **14**, Pt. 1, p.325.
1539 also. Powis (same places as in previous) (955) [SP.2/S ff.355-69]. See *L&P* **14**, Pt. 1, p.328.
1539 also. **Lordship of Caus**(land) (127) [SP.1/146 ff.175-78]. See *L&P* **14**, Pt. 1, p.324.
1546. Welshpool (109), **Hds.** of Deythur (164), **Caus** (222), **Mathrafal** (111), **Llanfyllin**(?) (358), **Pole** (204) [SP.1/226 f.154]. See *L&P* **21**, Pt. 2, pp.205-6.
1546. Hds. of Llanidloes Hd. (333), **Machynlleth** (262), **Newtown** (257), **Montgomery** (230) [SP.1/227 f.52]. See *L&P* **21**, Pt. 2, pp.205-6.
1639. Indenture roll (115; by hd.) [SP.16/419].

PEMBROKESHIRE

Public Record Office, Chancery Lane.

Muster Rolls
1539. Lordship of Haverfordwest and Dewisland. Tenants of Thomas Johns (380) [SP.2/S ff.316-41]. See *L&P* **14**, Pt. 1, p.324.
1539 also. **Lordship of Narberth** (144) [E.36/42 f.30]. 8pp. See *L&P* **14**, Pt. 1, p.327.
1539 also Cilgeran Hd. (250) [SP.2/S ff.342-49]. Good but very difficult hand. See *L&P* **14**, Pt. 1, p.324.
1640. Indenture roll (300) [SP.16/462].

RADNORSHIRE

Public Record Office, Chancery Lane.

Muster Rolls
1539. Town and Lordship of Presteign (146), **Lordships of Norton, Knighton and Knocklas** (137), **Town and Lordships of Radnor and Gladestry** (288), **Maelienydd** (437), **Gwrtheyrnion** (262) [E.36/20 f.59]. See *L&P* **14**, Pt. 1, p.327.
1539 also. **Lordships of Cynllaith-Owen** (Denb.) and **Stanage** (100) [E.36/20 f.54]. See *L&P* **14**, Pt. 1, p.327.
1640. Indenture roll (100; by hd.) [SP.16/462].

SCOTLAND

Records of musters up to the Act of Union of 1707 are at the **Scottish Record Office** in Edinburgh. The records of the Muster Master General survive in some quantity from 1681, with two earlier musters (1667 and 1675), and isolated lists from 1641, probably parliamentary records. They are well calendared by the S.R.O. with 41 references in Class E.100. Being somewhat outside the scope of this Guide, no further details are given here. Besides the names of the officers and soldiers in each company or troop, the rolls generally state the place and date of the muster. They are arranged in sections according to the regiment or garrison to which they belonged. Regiments were almost invariably known by the names of their Colonels or Commanding Officers for the time being. *The Scots Army, 1661-1688*, by C. Dalton (Edinburgh 1909) prints some of the muster rolls of the pre-union army.

Other muster rolls are scattered through a variety of collections of family papers, as are those for much of the rest of the eighteenth century. The Militia was only re-established in Scotland at the very end of the 18th century, but there were many less official bands of volunteer soldiers, particularly of course in 1745-46. Records of the re-established Militia are in the Public Record Office, Kew, but there are no earlier records in England.

The holdings of the Scottish Record Office are here divided chronologically into the period up to the Act of Union; and post-1707 to the later eighteenth century. They exclude those from the later eighteenth century on, which will be found in *Militia Lists and Musters*. As well as those in E.100, a few may relate to the Regular Army. Our own research has relied on catalogue entries rather than any physical examination, so some may not in fact include nominal rolls of any sort, though staff at the S.R.O. have gone to considerable trouble to check these for us. Further information will be welcome. Apart from the chronological grouping, the entries are left in the order of the individual family collections with no attempt at geographical arrangement.

Publications

Muster Roll of Prince Charles Edward Stuart's Army 1745-6, edited by C.W.H. Livingstone, C.W.H. Aikman and B.S. Hart (1984). Lists by Regiments about 5,900 names (some with age), occupation, residence and fate after battle.

Muster Roll for the Forfar or Lord Ogilvy's Regiment, raised on behalf of the Royal House of Stuart, 1745-6, by Alexander Mackintosh (Inverness, 1914). Lists alphabetically, as to rank, name, occupation, residence, parish, county and fate after battle. About 550 names with 65 biographical sketches of same.

Scottish Record Office, *Edinburgh.*

Seventeenth Century and to the Act of Union, 1707

Scrymgeour Wedderburn muniments
*c.*1640. Capt. John Scrymgeour's company at Montrose [GD.137/2128-9].

Hay of Haystoun papers
1641. Names of the ordinary yeomen of the guard [GD.34/896].

Glencairn muniments
1643. Roll of men and horses to be levied in **Renfrewshire** [GD.39/1/283].

Airlie muniments
1643. Fencible men on Earl of Airlie's lands [GD.16/50/17].
1644. Bond by Earl of Airlie's tenants to provide soldiers [GD.16/50/19].
1645. Prisoners at Philiphaugh [GD.16/50/24].
1648. Levy of men at Corsmiln to fight in expedition to England [GD.16/50/39].
1679-88. Muster rolls of Airlie troop [GD.16/51/9].

1644-48. Rolls of fencible persons, muster rolls, Kirk Yetholm and Morebattle [GD.6/1076].

Scott of Harden papers
1644-48. Rolls of fencible men in sheriffdom of **Selkirk** and parish of Yarrow [GD.157/1500].

Shairp of Houston muniments
1644-45. Roll and papers of Lieut. William Sharp's troop [GD.30/2056].
1692-99. Muster rolls of Capt. Walter Sharpe's company, Brigadier D'Offerrell's regt. [GD.30/2088].
1697-1701. Recruits, pay rolls, Col. Archibald Row's regt. [GD.30/2099-2106].
n.d. Fencible men in parish of Strabrock, West Lothian/Linlithgowshire [GD.30/2123].

Dalhousie muniments
1648. Letter with list of names, ?of those killed at Preston [GD.45/1/105].

Smythe of Methven papers
1650. Rolls of fencible men of Holme and Paplay [GD.190/2/192].

Lindsay of Dowhill muniments
1650. Rolls of fencible and unfencible men, Cleish [GD.254/679-80].

Fraser charters
1667. Muster roll of Sir Robert Dallzell's company [GD.86/662].
1689. Muster roll of Earl of Mar's company [GD.86/742].

Dalguise muniments
1672-85. Persons who kept their proportions of Lude's militia horse [GD.38/1/345].

Mar and Kellie papers
1680. Militia foot and horsemen due from each parish, **Aberdeenshire** [GD.124/13/19].
1685. Men from Earl of Mar's regt. in garrisons in S.W. Scotland [GD.124/13/37].

Stewart of Urrard papers
1681. List of men in the Marquis of Atholl's company [GD.1/394/76].

Society of Antiquaries of Scotland collection
1682-88. Muster rolls of Scots Guards [GD.103/2/209/4-6].
1687. Muster rolls of Earl of Mar's regt. [GD.103/2/209/1-3].

Elphinstone muniments [GD.156/Box 56/4].
1685. Roll of militia regiment of Stirling under Lord Elphinstone's command.
1690-1 and n.d. Rolls (2) of Lord Elphinstone's troop of horse, and pay accounts.
1693, 1695. Muster rolls and effective roll of Lord Elphinstone's company.

Messrs. Thomson, Dickson and Shaw, W.S., collection
*c.***1685.** Fencible men on estates of Marquis of Atholl [GD.241/380/10].

Kinross House papers
1688. Muster of West Militia regt. at **Kirkcaldy** [GD.29/49].

Leven and Melville papers
1690. Detailed regimental rolls of Earl of Argyll's regt. [GD.26/9/291].
*c.***1690.** Recruits, with companies [GD.26/9/304].
Late 17th cent. Dragoons in Capt. Hoom of Ninewalls' troop, Lord Cardross' regt. [GD.26/9/349].

Campbell of Jura papers
1690. Those in Mull who failed to surrender their arms to the Earl of Argyll [GD.64/2/29].

Campbell of Barcaldine papers
1692. Letter with 'list of the men and armes in the lands of Achnaba' [GD.170/611].

Montrose muniments
1705. Fencible men in the barony of **Buchanan** [GD.220/6/1598/18].

Eighteenth century, 1707 – 1770's

Leven and Melville papers
1708. Lists of the Artillery company in Scotland [GD.26/9/422].
1712. 'A list of the men discharged in August'; 'A list of the squades' [GD.26/9/466-7].
*c.***1750.** Detailed list of men in Lord Balgonie's company [GD.26/9/499].

Robertson of Kindeace papers
*c.***1713-97.** Muster rolls, *etc.* [GD.146/Box 18/1-2].

Biel muniments
1715. Men sent from Dirleton to keep guard at Seton [GD.6/1092]. Fencible men and militia foot soldiers in the parish of Dirleton [GD.6/1094-5].
1733. Roll of height and age of men in King's troop [GD.6/1098].

Clerk of Pencuik muniments
1715. List of some prisoners taken at Preston [GD.18/3158].
1733. Roll of height and age of men in King's troop [GD.6/1098].

Scotland: *Scottish Record Office* contd.

Sandilands of Eastbarns papers
1715. Capt. George Sandeland's company
[GD.1/382/36].

D. Murray Rose papers
1745. Sutherland Fencibles [GD.1/400/4/2].

Cardross writs
1746. Muster rolls of companies in Brig.
Gen. John Price's regt. of Foot, Fort
Augustus [GD.15/893/1/1-9].
1746. Muster rolls of companies in the
King's regt. of Foot commanded by Lieut.
Gen. Barrell, Fort Augustus
[GD.15/893/2/1-5].
1746. Muster roll of Capt. William
Cunningham's company, 2nd battalion,
Royal regt. of Foot, commanded by Lieut.
Gen. James St. Clair, Inverness
[GD.15/893/3].
1746. Muster roll of Capt. John Romer's
company, King's regt. of Foot, commanded
by Lt. Gen. Barrell [GD.15/894].

Rose of Kilravock muniments
?1746. Sick men in Lord John Murray's
Highlanders and other regts.
[GD.125/23/13/5].
1761. Muster rolls of Capt. William Rose's
company, Sutherland Highlanders
[GD.125/Box 24/1].

Craigmillar charters
1750. Pay rolls (2) of Capt. Little's company
of Militia [GD.122/3/17/40-1].

Ross Estate muniments
1762. Meeting of **Dumbartonshire** heritors
and freeholders to apply for establishment
of a militia [GD.47/371]. Lists heritors only.

Campbell of Balliveolan papers
1778. Attestations with personal details of
volunteers, Argyllshire Highland regt. of
Foot [GD.13/90].

Campbell of Barcaldine papers
1775-6. Recruits for Maj. Gen. Simon
Fraser's 71st regt. [GD.170/3435].
1778. Roll of Capt. James Campbell's
recruits [GD.170/3447-8].

CHANNEL ISLANDS: JERSEY

Publication
Muster lists: **1617.** St. Saviour; **1692.** St
Peter in *Societe Jersiaise Bulletin* **2**
(1885-9).

*La Societe Jersiaise, 9 Pier Road, St. Helier,
Jersey.*

Note. The collection is only partially
catalogued, and where documents are
undated only very approximate dating can
be suggested. Pre-19th century documents
are all ref. E.7/M.9.

Muster Lists
1617. St. Saviour. Published.
1692. St. Peter. Published.
1698. Unspecified military list (40).
n.d. (late 17th or early 18th cent.?). Fifth or
Herup company, 1st or North West regt.
(40).
1722, 1724, 1729. Capt. Charles de
Carteret's company (20 each).
n.d. (18th cent.). South regt. (1st, 2nd, 3rd,
4th companies, and artillery) (40 each).
n.d. (18th cent.). Fusilier company, Trinity
regt.

Note. There do not appear to be any relevant
records for Guernsey.